KAY D. RIZZO

Pacific Press Publishing Association
Boise, Idaho
Oshawa, Ontario, Canada

Special thanks to Helen Duewel, M.D.,
my physician, my medical counselor, my friend

And to my writing support system
Gwen, Brad, Trish, and Karen

Edited by Bonnie Widicker
Designed by Linda Griffith
Cover by James Maitland
Typeset in 10/12 Bookman

Library of Congress Catalog Card Number: 89-61519

ISBN 0-8163-0866-7

90 91 92 93 94 • 5 4 3 2 1

Table of Contents

Chapter 1

There Is a Season

"To every thing there is a season, and a time to every purpose under the heaven" (Ecclesiastes 3:1).

Kari paused in front of the brass-rimmed, full-length mirror in the hall of the Wynters' farmhouse and pushed a stray ebony curl back into the frazzled confines of the ponytail perched atop her head. Her eyes twinkled as she smiled. Just thinking about Marc made her feel warm inside.

She chuckled as she remembered the first time she'd met him. She had been standing alone on the deserted platform of the Columbus, Wisconsin, train depot. Frightened, she watched the only other detraining passenger disappear into the crowded station, wondering whether anyone would come for her. Startled by a voice behind her, she whirled about to find herself face to face with the third button of a well-filled chambray shirt. Lifting her gaze, she found herself staring into the most startlingly blue eyes she'd ever seen.

"And the rest is history," Kari giggled, then straightened her shoulders, assuming the mature pose of a proper farmer's wife.

"Kari Elaine Gerard, stop acting like a love-struck twelve-year-old," she scolded herself. "You are engaged, soon to be a married woman. Are you going to be such a romantic when you've been married twenty-five years?" The glint in her eyes said, "If I have my way . . ."

Suddenly she remembered her assignment—find Marc and his sister Shelly. Tell them that the homemade ice cream had been frozen and was ready to be devoured.

5

Kari understood that Marc and Shelly, the two oldest of the four Wynters children, had always been close. It was not unusual for them to sequester themselves away in the family room for a catch-up chat whenever Shelly, her husband John, and their two children visited from Michigan. The only child of an unwed mother, Kari envied them that bond. She hoped that in time, she and Shelly could form a similar relationship like real sisters.

The thick beige carpet absorbed the sound of Kari's footsteps as she hurried toward the family room. Just before reaching the doorway, she heard Shelly say her name.

"Marc, I'm not saying I don't like Kari. She's a good girl. Mom and Dad can't sing her praises enough, I assure you."

Kari paused, uncertain whether or not to proceed.

"Then what's the problem?" Marc sounded irritated. "I love Kari very much. I'm not interested in any other woman."

"Little brother, how many girls have you dated seriously—say, since high school?"

"Seriously?"

"Seriously!"

Kari wavered. She had three choices—eavesdrop, make noise so Marc and Shelly would know she was near, or turn and run. Marc spoke before she could decide.

"You know the answer, Shelly. I had to study too hard during college to date seriously. It wasn't until I met Yvonne in my last year that I felt I could do justice to a relationship. By then I'd met Kari, and well," Marc chuckled, "Yvonne never really had a chance."

Kari's eyes misted, and she felt the warm glow again.

From within the room, Shelly continued. "I rest my case."

"Look, sis, Kari and I are not exactly children, you know. I'm twenty-four; she's twenty-one."

"I don't question your maturity, little brother. It's Kari's immaturity that worries me. Making a marriage work is tough at best. And as mature as Kari might be mentally and physically, she's—she's such a babe in so many ways." Shelly paused. "She's had a rough time of it. She needs time to heal emotionally from the scars of her past. More important, she needs time to mature spiritually. I suspect Kari has spiritual battles to fight that you and I will never be able to understand. Give her time to catch up with you a bit."

Tears welled up in Kari's eyes. "I can't go in there now," she thought. The squeak of a spring jolted her to action. Someone had risen from the sofa. Kari whirled about, looking for an escape, any escape.

The screen door clattered behind her as she ran out the front door and down the porch steps. Reaching the safety of her '68 Chevy before giving in to tears, she groped blindly toward the ignition to start the engine. "Oh, no," she wailed, banging her fists against the steering wheel, "the keys are in my purse in the kitchen. I give up!"

She flung the car door open and climbed out onto the gravel driveway. As she slammed the car door behind her, she glanced toward the house and caught a glimpse of Marc's surprised face in the family room window.

Not wanting him to question her tears or to know that she'd been eavesdropping, Kari strode down the long driveway toward the main road. She hurried past the field of waist-high corn on her left and Mom Wynters' blossoming rose bushes on her right.

A gentle breeze stirred the leaves of the trees lining the roadway in an attempt to ease the stifling humidity of the July day. She heard the screen door open and Marc's voice.

"Kari? Where are you off to?"

"Feel like taking a walk," she said without turning around. She prayed that her voice wouldn't betray her emotions.

"Want some company?"

They'd walked the country lane together many times during their stormy two-year courtship.

"I'd like to be alone for a few minutes," she called without breaking her stride. It was only after she heard the screen door slam that she glanced back toward the white farmhouse. No one was in sight. She'd gotten her way, but was it what she really wanted?

So many times in her life, Kari hadn't been sure just what it was she had wanted. Becoming a Christian? Yes, she had definitely wanted that extra something her friend and spiritual mentor, Amanda Fisher, possessed. Training as a licenced practical nurse? Yes, that too—possibly more to please Amanda. Leaving Chicago to move to Beaver Dam,

Wisconsin? Well . . . it had seemed like the best move at the time. Forced to chose between resisting her mother's boyfriend's sexual advances or leaving Chicago, Kari had taken Amanda's offer to spend the summer on a dairy farm owned by Amanda's sister and brother-in-law.

When she first arrived at the Wynters' home, Kari discovered a caring family—friends that would give her the peace and security she so desperately craved. Yet she also found this new life to be anything but peaceful or secure. Instead, her heart and her carefully planned life went topsy-turvy from her very first view of that third button.

Kari swatted at a pesky mosquito staking claim on her bare arm. "Marc. His irresistible blue eyes. His lovable smile and his compelling nature. Oh yes, his compelling nature!"

For the most part, she'd been loved into the Wynters' hearts. Mom treated her as a third daughter from the moment she entered the sprawling farmhouse. Dad Wynters, slightly less demonstrative, understood what Kari had been through and slowly broke through the girl's reserve. Michael and Mindy, Marc's younger siblings, stood in awe of her every move. In their eyes, she could do no wrong. Only Shelly remained aloof—kind, cordial, yet aloof.

As she walked, Kari reviewed word by word the conversation she'd overheard. "I thought she liked me. I thought we just needed time to get acquainted, what with her living in Michigan and all." Kari angled across the road to the ancient, gnarled tree atop the road bank at the edge of the driveway. She climbed the bank and sat down on an exposed root.

"Not mature enough spiritually?" Kari tucked her knees up under her chin. "When Yvonne showed up, didn't I back off? Didn't I leave Marc and my relationship in God's hands? Doesn't that show spiritual maturity?"

She stared down the corridor of corn before her. "Perhaps she thinks I'm not good enough for her little brother—poor, abused, converted heathen straight off the city streets." Mosquitos buzzed about her head as Kari wallowed in her misery. She flung her hands about, trying to discourage the hungry pests. The insects' persistence triggered a new, stronger emotion in Kari. Jumping to her feet, she straightened her shoulders and lifted her chin defiantly.

"I refuse to let her defeat me! I'll show her and everyone else. I'll be the best Christian wife anyone could ask for!" Kari swiped at the moist streaks staining her face. A new thought caused her to start. "If Marc hasn't changed his mind about marrying me."

She and Marc had been engaged since April but had never formally set the date until the previous evening, when they'd ostensibly been checking the hay crop in the field next to the river. September 30—the couple had planned to announce it to the family that evening, after returning from the Fourth of July fireworks.

Doubts niggled at Kari's mind, puncturing her already shaky self-esteem. "What if Mom and Dad feel the same as Shelly? Maybe I am only a little missionary project to them too. I should come right out and ask!" Even as she voiced her thoughts to the restless audience of immature cornstalks, she knew she'd never take the risk of knowing.

"If Marc changes his mind, what will he do with the farm we just bought?" When Kari and Marc took out a mortgage on the farm next door to the Wynters' property, she had moved into the old farmhouse and begun redecorating to her and her fiancé's tastes. She'd enjoyed sewing ruffled curtains for the kitchen, wallpapering and painting the bedroom in her spare time from working at the Beaver Dam Hospital. "I suppose I would have to move into town if we broke up." She felt pain at the thought of leaving the little country cottage she'd grown to think of as home—her very first real home.

Steadying herself against the tree trunk, she once again relived the disturbing conversation. She ignored a scolding blackbird high on a branch above her head. She barely noticed the steady orchestration of chirping insects serenading her. A grasshopper plopped on the toe of her left sneaker, then continued on his journey to a tuft of grass beside her.

"Well," she admitted, "I can't stay out here forever. Sooner or later I have to go back and act as if nothing has happened."

Reluctantly, she returned to the house. After a quick visit to the bathroom to splash cold water on her face, she pasted a smile on her face and strolled toward the sound of happy voices coming from the back porch.

When Kari stepped out onto the porch, she glanced about at the holiday scene before her. Michael and Marc stood on the lawn near the ice-cream freezer. Shelly's two children, four-year-old Jennifer and two-year-old Josh, sat sandwiched between Mom and Dad Wynters on the porch swing. Kari avoided looking toward Shelly, perched on the porch railing beside her husband, John.

Cross-legged on the grass, Mindy inhaled giant mouthfuls of freshly blended strawberry ice cream. "Where've ya' been?" Mindy cocked her head to one side.

Kari avoided Marc's questioning gaze. "I took a walk. I felt a headache coming on."

Michael dropped a huge scoop of ice cream into a large cereal bowl and started to hand it to Kari.

"Hey, wait a minute," Mindy objected, her eyes twinkling devilishly. "Remember the story of the little red hen."

Kari frowned. "The little red hen?"

"Oh, yes, a tradition in the Wynters' family. You don't know the story of the little red hen?" Mindy teased.

"Now, Mindy," Marc cautioned, "I'm sure Kari—"

"Oh no! Since she's soon to become a genuine member of the Wynters' clan, she has to accept her obligations as a true Wynters."

"Look who's talking," Michael interrupted. "The expert at escaping manual labor of any kind."

Everyone laughed, including Kari. "OK, so what does this little red hen have to do with a bowl of ice cream?"

"Mama," Mindy coaxed, "you tell her the story."

Jennifer nodded excitedly. "Yes, Grandma, tell us the story."

Mom Wynters tucked the four-year-old into the crook of her arm. "Well, once there was a little red hen who decided to make some bread." Mom continued her story about the farm animals, who, when asked to help the hen with the bread-making process, refused. "So when the hen removed the loaves of bread from the oven and the delicious aromas wafted across the barnyard, the animals each wanted a slice of her bread. But the little red hen refused. "Since you wouldn't help me make the bread, you can't help me eat it."

"So, since you didn't help—" Mindy teased.

"Well, for all the help you gave, you're sure getting more than your share," Michael defended, handing Kari the bowl of ice cream. "Here, don't pay any attention to her."

Kari laughed. "How about if I help clean up this mess? Does that count?" she volunteered.

"Hey." Mindy's eyes brightened at the suggestion. "Sounds like a good deal to me."

Marc bounded up the porch steps to Kari's side. "And I'll help." He slid his arm protectively about her waist. "Might be fun. But first, Kari and I have an announcement to make." He squeezed her reassuringly.

"Now, Marc?" Kari started, searching his eyes for signs of doubt or insincerity.

"Now! We've set our wedding date for September 30." Marc planted a reassuring kiss on Kari's cheek.

While Shelly watched, the rest of the family enthusiastically congratulated the couple. In between kisses and hugs, Kari glanced toward Shelly. Shelly cast a tentative smile toward Kari. She struggled to return the gesture.

"Oh," Mindy stopped in astonishment, "we've so much to do."

"We?" Marc snorted. "You, little sister?"

Mindy stomped her foot impatiently. "Yes, we! Don't worry, I'll do my share!"

"Hmmph!" Michael snorted. "That will be the day!"

In the weeks to come, Mindy surprised everyone with her willingness to help with the wedding preparations. The month of July disappeared amid a swirl of gossamer, Belgian lace, and string beans. Preparations for both the wedding and the coming winter invaded every room of the house.

In the kitchen, freshly filled canning jars vied for shelf space with ripening vegetables. In the family room and upstairs bedrooms, diaphanous gowns of pinks and lavenders, with their corresponding scraps, lay strewn about in delightful disarray.

Kari worked side by side with Mindy and Mom, sewing hems and paring fruit during the day while maintaining her nightly nursing schedule at the local hospital. On the graveyard shift, while her patients slept, she addressed wedding invitations. Janet, the nurse's aide assigned to Kari's ward, frequently pitched in to help.

"What ever happened to throwing old-fashioned rice?" Janet asked one evening as the two women sat in the nurses' station assembling pink net-covered birdseed packets.

"People say," Kari began, "that after the birds eat the rice, the rice swells inside of them and kills them."

"Aw, come on," Janet scoffed.

"That's what they say," Kari defended. "Do you want the guilt of hundreds of dead, bloated bird bodies on your conscience?"

Janet snorted her disbelief and tossed the packet she'd been working on into the partially filled grocery bag. "So much for tradition."

"Tradition!" Kari tugged at the crinkle ribbon that seemed determined to slip stubbornly from her fingers. "I can't believe all the traditions associated with weddings. A simple wedding—that's all Marc and I really want."

Janet nodded. "I know what you mean. What starts out as a private love affair between two people somehow mushrooms into a Hollywood extravaganza."

Kari sighed. "Sometimes, I think it would be so much easier to elope or maybe just call it off—head for the north woods or something."

"Getting cold feet?" Janet looked around at the wedding clutter surrounding them. "I wouldn't if I were you. There just might be a lynching if you try it."

Kari grabbed her throat in mock alarm. "Oh no, call in Perry Mason—'The Case of the Runaway Bride.' Seriously, with all the flurry at home, I wouldn't be surprised if the groom cut and ran."

"Oh, ho ho," Janet laughed. "Fat chance. I've never seen a more attentive bridegroom than Marc."

Kari blushed. Her friend was right. Marc had been so patient and caring through all of the commotion. Instead, Kari was the one becoming increasingly nervous the closer she came to September 30.

Exhaustion, the hated conversation between Marc and Shelly, fears that Shelly might even be right disturbed her continually. Kari's days merged into her nights, forming one long train of wedding preparation. She hardly knew where one night ended and the next day began. The fittings, her work at the hospital, the nonending round of parties and trips to town for odds and ends were taking their toll on her energy supply. Kari was certain that her puffy eyelids would forever remain at half-mast.

The ten-mile drive home from work each morning was the worst. Some mornings, her battered-up old Chevy seemed to possess a high-technology homing device. "And somewhere in this madness," she reminded herself, "I need to find time for Marc—and for me."

One morning, as the car eased to a stop in front of their soon-to-be honeymoon haven, Kari leaned back against the car seat. "I'm too exhausted to even get out of the car."

The August sun beating down soon forced Kari to stumble from the car and into the cool, dark interior of the house. After taking a tepid shower, she wrapped a bath towel about her and crossed the hall into the master bedroom.

She gazed about the freshly wallpapered room and smiled. The pastel shades of pink, yellow, and cream from the wallpaper brought out the same shades in the four delicate English floral prints she'd picked up at a garage sale and reframed and hung above the massive four-poster bedstead. She ran her hand over the arm of the antique rosewood rocker beside the bed.

"Someday," she predicted, "I'll rock our babies to sleep in this chair . . . sleep . . . that sounds s-o-o-o good right now."

As she slipped into her cotton plissé nightie, she noticed her Bible resting on the night stand by the bed and winced. It's been a while, she admitted. She knelt beside the bed and whispered a perfunctory prayer. Kari tumbled into the bed, knowing she'd babble the same empty clichés when she awoke in a few hours.

When she took the time to think about it, a hunger gnawed at her—not a hunger for physical food, but for spiritual nourishment. I've got to spend more time with God, she reasoned. But how? When? Her head sank into the plump, downy pillow. "Do all brides go though this madness?"

Chapter 2
A Time to Hate

Marc playfully brushed aside a stray curl and kissed Kari's neck. She smiled and shrugged her shoulder against her cheek. "Marc, be serious. We need to talk."

"I am being serious," he replied, as he intently studied her neck. "You have the tiniest earlobes I've ever seen."

"Marc . . ." Kari's tone deepened into a mild threat. "What are we going to do about purchasing a tractor for the place? Those beauties are humongously expensive!"

Marc laughed and leaned back against the chintz-covered couch. "Humongous? You've been hanging around Mindy too much lately." He stretched his long, blue-jeaned legs out onto the maple-stained coffee table. All the while, his left hand continued to draw invisible spirals on his fiancée's neck.

"Marc, please." Kari slid to the far end of the sofa. "This is important. We can't expect to operate our place indefinitely, using your dad's machinery."

"OK, OK. I'll be serious." Marc heaved a huge sigh. "I talked with Mr. Morton at the bank yesterday about taking out an additional loan in order to purchase some used farm equipment. He also suggests we insure our crops. But that would involve putting out bucks we don't have."

"Do your parents buy crop insurance?"

Marc nodded. "They try to cover at least a portion of their yearly yield."

"It makes sense."

"I suppose," Marc drawled. "We have an appointment to talk with Mr. Morton tomorrow afternoon around four."

"Tomorrow at four?" Kari replied impatiently. "Your mother

14

and I have to be at the florist then. There you go, being high-handed again. If you'd told me sooner, I could have arranged another time."

"I'm sorry," Marc answered, his lips tightening into a thin line. "It's the only time Mr. Morton had free on his calendar until next week. You did say getting a used tractor was a high-priority item, didn't you?"

Marc's even tones irked Kari further. "Well, so is choosing the flowers for the wedding. You do want flowers, don't you?"

Studiously, he smoothed the back of Kari's rumpled collar. "Of course," he coaxed, unaware of the effect his conde-scending manner had on Kari's strung-out nerves.

"Marc," she snapped, "it doesn't matter to you that you plan my every waking moment without thought of consulting me, does it?"

"Hey! All I did was—"

"All you did was fill up my already too full day without—"

Marc ran his fingers through his hair in frustration. "Look, all I did was do exactly as you requested last week, and now I'm being accused—"

"That's right, blame me. It's always my fault."

Kari hadn't finished reciting her long list of supposed and real complaints before Marc threw his hands into the air and shouted, "Whoa! What are we arguing about anyway?"

"I-I-I," Kari stuttered, "I told you. You are always telling me what to do. I am always having to adjust my life to fit yours!"

"If that's so, then I'm sorry. I'll call Mr. Morton the first thing in the morning and arrange for an appointment for sometime next week, OK? Are you satisfied?"

Kari juggled her foot in irritation and picked at the yarn pills on the multicolored afghan covering the back of the couch. "That's not the point I am trying to make. I'll go to the bank with you. It's just . . . just . . . oh, I don't know," she wailed. "This wedding thing is out of control. I'm so tired I could . . ."

Before she could finish, Marc pulled her into the protec-tion of his strong arms. "There, there," he murmured, bury-ing his face in her ebony curls. "You're trying to be some kind of super woman. Canning, sewing, fixing up our new home, and working full time. Come on, kid." He reached to the box of tissues sitting on the coffee table. "Here."

"Thanks," she sniffed. "But what else can I do? There is so much to be done before the wedding."

"You could pass the work around. Let Mindy and Michael do some of the running around. And evenings, I can help."

"You're already working long days."

Marc lifted her tear-stained face to his and kissed the tip of her reddened nose. "Hey, we're a team now, remember?" He searched her dark, luminous eyes questioningly. "There's still something wrong. Are you keeping anything from me?"

A fresh barrage of tears cascaded down her face as she crumpled against his gray shirt. "My mother called this morning. She's not coming to the wedding."

"Why? Does she lack the money?"

"I don't know. She didn't say."

Marc remained silent as Kari cried out her frustrations. When her tears subsided, he spoke. "Why don't we take a drive down to see her this weekend? She may change her mind if she knows just how much you'd like her to be at the wedding."

"Oh, Marc, we can't. Mindy and I are planning on putting up bush beans on Friday. And besides, the annual teen picnic and hayride is this weekend. We really should be there since we're the sponsors."

"I think your mom is more important than a church outing or a pot of string beans. We're not indispensable," Marc reminded. "Mindy and Mom can handle the beans—and I'll get Jack and Sylvia Barron to sponsor the group."

"It would be kind of nice to get away from everything for a few days," Kari admitted. "Besides, you've never spent much time with my mother. She should get to know you better before the wedding." An unexpected frown filled Kari's face. "Then again, maybe that isn't such a great idea."

Marc laughed, rocking Kari back and forth in his arms. "After all the talking you and I have done during the last two years, I doubt this weekend will hold many surprises."

"You don't know my mother," she warned.

When they arrived on Friday afternoon, Kari's mother lay on the couch in a drunken stupor in spite of the advanced notice they had given. Kari glanced about the untidy room.

Much had changed since her last visit—for the worse. Fighting to control her revulsion, Kari stepped gingerly around the discarded wine bottles, beer cans, and dirty clothing to reach her mother's side. Kari's stomach lurched at the smell of dried vomit and sweat when she bent down to kiss her mother on the cheek. Kari studiously avoided looking at Marc, afraid to see his reaction.

"Mom, how could you do this to me?" Kari thought, her spine rigid with censure. "How many times have I come home to this?"

Aloud, Kari said, "Sheena, you remember my fiancé, Marc?"

Sheena lifted her head unsteadily from the soiled sofa pillow and slurred, "Huh? Oh, yeah, your fancy-pants, college graduate, farm boy."

"Please, Mom, let's not get the weekend off to a bad start."

Pointing a shaky finger in her daughter's face, Sheena growled, "Sheena, the name's Sheena, remember? I didn't invite you here. You ran off to the farm with this hayseed, not the other way around, you know."

"That's ancient history, right?"

"So why are you here, anyway? Surely you don't want this wine sot to stain the atmosphere of your pristine wedding."

Kari started at her mother's vehemence. "Of course I want you at my wedding. You're my mother, remember?"

Marc set down the luggage he'd been holding and hurried to Sheena's side. "Mrs. Gerard, we both want you at our wedding."

Kneeling beside the couch, he touched the woman's emaciated arm. An empty fold of skin, translucent and wrinkled, hung from Sheena's forearm as she tried to wave him away. The dark circles beneath her haunted eyes intensified her unsettling stare.

"You're not feeling well, are you?" He touched her sweaty forehead.

"Give the horse doctor an A," she mocked. "If I were feeling well, I'd be out partying!"

"Sheena!" Kari snapped.

Marc turned toward Kari. "Your mother needs medical attention. Who is your family doctor?"

"Family doctor? You must be joking!" Kari laughed. "The Women's Free Clinic on Fourth Street will have to do."

He touched Sheena's forehead, his professional gaze skimmed the woman's anorexic form. "Her temperature is elevated. She needs medical attention immediately."

Suddenly the fight drained from Sheena's face. She allowed Kari and Marc to help her into fresh clothing. Tears filled Kari's eyes as she ran a hairbrush through the thin, dull strands of her mother's orange-dyed, frizzled hair. "How could this happen?" she wondered. "A woman who always took such pride in her looks wasting away to this?"

At the clinic, Kari and Marc waited while Sheena submitted to the necessary examination. Later, Sheena didn't demure about the couple being present to hear the physician's diagnosis.

Marc squeezed Kari's hand tenderly as Dr. Scott made her report.

"Unfortunately, with cirrhosis of the liver, the symptoms don't appear until the disease has made serious headway in the body. Acute malnutrition often confuses the diagnosis." She paused in her explanation. "Cirrhosis is a hardening of the liver due to an increase in connective tissue and degeneration of the active liver cells—like scar tissue. As you know, alcohol is one of the leading causes."

Kari nodded.

"This will explain the disease further." She handed Kari a tri-folded pamphlet. "Inside you'll find an outline of the regimen your mother will need to follow to regain her strength. While we can't eradicate the disease, we can enrich and prolong her life and perhaps prevent secondary infections from ending it." The physician shook her finger at Sheena. "But most and foremost, no more liquor of any kind!"

Back at the apartment, it took hours of persuasion to convince Sheena to return with Kari to the farmhouse in Wisconsin. "I am a nurse, Mother. Caring for sick people is my business, remember?"

"Only until the wedding," Sheena stipulated, allowing her daughter to tuck the bedcovers under her chin, "then I come back home. Do you understand? Newlyweds need to be alone. They don't need a mother-in-law around."

"We'll cross that bridge when we come to it," Kari soothed. When Marc suggested driving across town to see his Aunt Amanda before leaving the city, Kari welcomed the opportunity to straighten her mother's apartment.

She bustled around the parlor, tossing her mother's dirty and discarded clothing into garbage bags. Tears stung her eyes as she paused at the bedroom door and listened to her mother's labored breathing. Kari filled her arms with empty bottles, cans, and glassware, then dumped them onto the kitchen counter next to the sink. After sorting and discarding all trash, she began washing dishes.

Dipping her hands into the hot, sudsy dish water eased Kari's tension. One after another, she washed and rinsed the cracked, mismatched dishware. Idly, she picked up a glass tumbler, partially filled with a dark, translucent liquid and held it up to the light. She smiled ruefully, remembering the times as a teenager she'd finished her mother's discarded drinks while washing dishes. She recalled the soothing sensation of the tepid liquid slipping down her throat and the warm, numbing sense of security that always followed.

"I could sure use a little assurance right now," Kari admitted. She turned the glass in her hand, watching the light filter through the amber shadows.

The front door slammed. "Hi, honey, I'm back."

Startled, Kari dropped the tumbler. It caught on the edge of the porcelain sink and shattered, sending its contents across the counter, up and down the cupboard doors, and on Kari.

"Wow, things sure look better in here." Marc strolled into the kitchen. "Amanda and the kids send their love and understood why you couldn't come over. She also volunteered to finish cleaning the apartment for you so that we can get an early start back."

Kari closed her eyes and leaned heavily against the counter. "You gave me a start. I didn't hear you come up the stairs."

"I'm sorry." Marc surveyed the damage. "Did I make you do that? Careful, you'll cut yourself, honey. Let me clean up the broken glass while you get your mom ready to leave."

Chapter 3

A Time to Love

Kari yawned and stretched, her entire body drugged with a drowsy warmth. Without opening her eyes, she could feel the early morning sunlight playing a coy game of hide-and-seek with the intricate lace patterns of the white curtains at her bedroom window. A cooling breeze skittered across the bed, caressing her sleepy eyelids. She responded by burrowing farther beneath the soft, downy quilt. The bedroom door opened, and the smell of homemade waffles teased her awake.

Her eyes focused on the yards and yards of white gossamer suspended from the hook on the back of the closet door—her wedding gown. Her wedding day!

Kari bolted from the bed. "What time is it? Did I oversleep?"

Sheena stood in the doorway, breakfast tray in hand. "Hey, you have plenty of time. I wanted to serve my beautiful daughter breakfast in bed on her wedding day."

Kari grabbed the alarm clock from the night stand and gasped, "It's already 7:30. I have so much to do."

"And to begin with, get back into bed so I can put this tray down."

Kari stared in disbelief at her smiling mother, then at the tray of food. Sheena had made her breakfast, breakfast in bed. Obediently, Kari settled herself in the middle of the bed and smoothed the covers into place. Her eyes misted as she watched her mother place the tray on the bed, then flutter about, adjusting the silverware and filling her glass with orange juice.

"I hope everything is the way you like it." Sheena's eyes begged for Kari's approval. "I've never made Bavarian waffles before. It wasn't so bad really, kind of fun, in fact."

Kari choked back her tears. The six weeks since Kari and Marc returned from Chicago had been like a dream for her. With good food and exercise, Sheena regained her health in record time. In addition, mother and daughter had come to know and understand each other as never before.

There had been rough times when Sheena's disease-ridden body screamed for the soporific poison of alcohol, forcing Kari to her knees to beg for strength to resist her mother's tirades and tears. Yet, it had been good. In spite of the wedding preparations, her job at the hospital, and the added responsibility of her mother's health, Kari decided it had been good. She had felt the need to pray again, to claim the promises that had been so important to her in the beginning. Promises such as Isaiah 40:31: "They that wait upon the Lord shall renew their strength; they shall mount up with wings as eagles." She'd felt the strength of eagles again, both physically and spiritually.

The best part was Sheena's hunger for spiritual food too. Her mother had actually been eager to learn and to believe. Yes, "all things do work together for good," Kari decided.

"Kari?" Sheena laughed. "Anyone home? I know brides are supposed to be a little distracted, but I've been talking to the breeze for at least five minutes now."

"Huh? Oh, I'm sorry."

"Your waffles are getting soggy."

Kari attacked the first of the plump, sugar-coated straw-berries.

"Now I know you were probably saving those strawberries for winter, but I couldn't resist." Sheena's eagerness to please her daughter bubbled out with every gesture.

"It's delicious, Sheena. Thank you so much." Kari stared at the overabundance of food before her. "But you'll have to help me eat this, or I won't be able to get into my gown this afternoon. And boy, will Mom Wynters be frustrated, after all the fittings she put me through."

A whisper of a cloud passed across Sheena's face. "Kari, I never wanted you to call me 'mother.' It always made me feel so old." The woman paused, her fingers following the wedding-ring patterns in the bed quilt. "I've changed my mind. Would you? Could, could you call me, Mom, just once, even if I don't really deserve it?"

A cry escaped Kari's throat as she reached for her mother's shoulders. "Oh, Mom, I love you so much. You just gave me the most precious wedding gift you could have given me. Thank you so much." Tears streamed as the two women clung to each other despite the precariously balanced food tray.

Kari and her mother broke apart as icy cold orange juice spilled onto the quilt and into their laps. "Oh," Sheena squealed, "I'm sorry. I'm so sorry. Orange juice all over your beautiful new wedding quilt."

Giggles arose unbidden from deep within Kari until the entire bed shook with her laughter. "Who cares?" she gasped between bouts of hysteria. "What's a little OJ between a daughter and her mother?"

"Kari Gerard," Sheena chuckled, grabbing the tray and setting it on the rocking chair beside the bed, "that makes no sense at all."

"I know!" Kari held her juice-stained nightgown out from her body with two fingers and with the other hand, pointed at Sheena's equally stained blouse. "That's why it's so funny."

"You're a nut case! Are you sure Marc knows what a weirdo he's marrying?"

When Kari thought of the staid and steady Marc waking to a shower of orange juice, she broke into a fresh round of hilarity. "If he doesn't, he soon will!"

Their laughter almost drowned out the sound of honking horns outside in the front yard. Kari bounded to the window just in time to see Mindy and Amanda hop out of Amanda's Ford station wagon.

"Hey, sleepyhead." Mindy waved. "We've come to take your stuff to the church. Mom and the other ladies are already decorating the church and the reception hall."

Kari dashed down the stairs and met them at the front door. "But I have orders that you are not to show your face there until noon. Here is your lemon verbena bubble bath, and . . ." Mindy's eyes traveled over Kari's soiled nightgown. "I see you've already eaten breakfast."

"It's a long story," Kari giggled feebly.

"And interesting, to be sure," Mindy added, sweeping past Kari and up the stairs to the bedroom. "But right now we're on a strict schedule."

From the upstairs hall, Mindy continued. "Marc is as nervous as a polecat at a hounddog convention. Mom had to ban him from the house."

"I'll hurry and get dressed," Kari began.

"You'll do no such thing." Amanda grabbed Kari by the shoulders and gently led her to the sofa. "Your job is to relax, to think serenity. A serene bride is a beautiful bride. Sheena, don't let her frazzle herself into a tizzy this morning."

The morning disappeared in a whirlwind of nervous energy despite Amanda's instructions. By the time Kari reached the small white clapboard chapel, any calm she might have acquired had vanished.

As she entered the dressing area, she greeted each of her attendants with a nervous kiss. When she reached Shelly, she forced a smile and kissed Marc's older sister on the cheek.

Crinolines, hoops, ruffles, and lace swooshed about the dressing area amidst a buzz of whispers and nervous giggles. A bevy of female relatives, a photographer, and a hairstylist fluttered around Kari. But the moment Amanda, the matron of honor, placed the pearl-encrusted crown with its frothy netting on Kari's dark, lustrous curls, everyone gasped in awe.

Kari stared at the stranger in the oval mirror. The thickly fringed, luminous green eyes, the slightly tilted nose, and cloud of raven hair belonged to another. Her flawless blush spoke of a woman in love. Amanda reverently lowered the whisper-fine veil over Kari's face.

Mom Wynters sniffled shamelessly into her handkerchief while Sheena turned to camouflage the evidence of her happiness. Tears brimmed in Kari's eyes, threatening to fall onto her white satin bodice.

Shelly rushed to her side and shook her gently. "Oh, no you don't, Kari soon-to-be-Wynters. You are not going to marry my brother with red, puffy eyes!" Everyone laughed, effectively breaking the tension.

Kari glanced up at Shelly. "Who has the red, puffy eyes— me or Marc?"

"Probably both of you, the way Marc's been acting all morning!"

Kari allowed the photographer to pose her with first one attendant, then another. Occasionally she caught a glimpse of her mother, hands folded, fingertips to her lips as if in prayer. Tears glistened in Sheena's eyes as she took in the festivities.

From the moment the organist hit the first chord of the wedding march, Kari's mind blanked. She moved through the practiced steps in a trance. Even the noise and excitement of the reception line barely reached her inner mind.

"My beautiful, beautiful wife," Marc whispered as he lifted a goblet of sparkling cider to her lips.

They were still admiring the vast array of wedding gifts when Amanda suggested Kari change into her going-away suit. Together, the two women slipped away from the throng to the dressing area. Sheena followed.

As Kari tucked the apricot silk blouse under the waistband of her white linen suit, Sheena smoothed imaginary wrinkles from the shoulders of Kari's suit jacket. "You know, I never had a wedding, never thought I'd want one. Your dad and I, well, we never even . . ."

Kari looked at her mother with new, more compassionate eyes. "I know."

"I've had a rough life, lots of troubles, most I brought on myself. But seeing you today made it all worth it." Sheena paused and bit her lip. "Kari, you are the only beautiful thing, the only good thing in my entire life. Thank you for insisting I be a part of your day."

Kari sniffed and reached for her mother.

Sheena shook her head and grabbed her daughter's hands in her own. "Now, don't go getting soppy on me. You've got one terrific guy out there who's very much in love with you. Go to him. Be happy."

"Oh, Mama, I will, I will. I'll be the best wife any woman can be. You wait, you'll see."

Chapter 4
A Time to Rend

Kari handed Marc her travel case and leaped from the boat onto an exposed tree root. Marc set the case on the bank and slipped his arm protectively about her waist. She scanned the quiet waters of Castle Rock Lake. "I hate to leave all of this behind. Do you think we'll ever return?"

"How about on our twenty-fifth anniversary?" He placed a teasing kiss on her upturned nose and brushed his fingertips along her chinline.

"Sooner than that, I hope!" she added emphatically.

The island cottage, eating s'mores by campfire, early morning walks on leaf-strewn trails of Indian summer, a wild ride down the Wisconsin Dells, even a visit to a genuine Indian reservation shaped a montage of tender memories for the honeymooning couple. But there was a harvest to complete, cattle to feed, and the chill from the pending Wisconsin winter that lingered longer and longer each morning.

Even though she'd dreaded leaving their honeymoon haven, Kari also felt a tingle of excitement building. Somehow, the wedding and the week-long honeymoon seemed more like playing house. She eagerly anticipated building their lives together in the real world.

Within minutes their car was loaded and heading south toward home. Kari inserted a cassette into the tape deck and settled back for the long drive home. Resting her hand comfortably on Marc's knee, she watched the gently rolling hills speeding by. Marc tapped out the rhythm of the a cappella singing group on the steering wheel. "I wonder how your mother is doing back in Chicago?"

"Hey, we're married," Kari laughed. "I was just thinking the same thing."

"Do you think she might have taken my mother's invitation to stay at their place for a while?"

"I doubt it. She's very independent. After all, she's been on her own since she was nine years old."

"She's had a rough life, all right."

Kari nodded. "Four generations of alcohol abuse. I'm so glad I escaped."

Marc glanced over at Kari, his eyes tender with compassion. "Me too."

As they passed each familiar waymark, Kari's excitement grew. She'd had little time at the reception to appreciate their wedding gifts. It would be like an early Christmas going through their gifts at her leisure, deciding where each would be stored, and writing thank-you notes to all of their friends. By the time Marc eased the car onto the gravel driveway leading to their house, Kari had unlatched her seatbelt, her hand resting on the door handle.

"Hey, wait until the car stops, will ya'?" Marc teased. "Besides, I have to carry the bride across the threshold."

Settling into a routine proved to be as delightful as Kari had anticipated. She and Marc had agreed she'd take a break from working at the hospital until there was an opening on a shift other than graveyard's eleven to seven. This gave her time to do all the little housewifely things she'd dreamed about doing.

She poured over each month's homemaker magazines for new recipes to try. With Mom Wynters' help, she learned to operate the antiquated treadle sewing machine that had come with the house. She made tablecloths, aprons, dresses, and an occasional shirt for Marc.

Each morning, after cleaning up the kitchen, she couldn't resist taking an extra peek at the multicolored rows of glass jars filled with string beans, peaches, corn, cherries, blackberry jam—the bounty of the previous summer's hard work—lining the pantry shelves. And as the cold November winds rattled the windowpanes of the little farmhouse, she and Marc would spend the evening, he at his desk, working on the farm ledgers, and she, curled up on the couch, figuring out the intricacies of "knit one, purl one." Regardless of how tight their budget might be, Kari felt wealthy beyond belief. When a tiny little bundle of gray fluff mysteriously appeared on their doorstep during the first snowstorm of the winter, their home was complete. Swietzer, a long-haired Burmese kitten, immediately won a place in their hearts and home.

The newlyweds threw themselves into all the church and community affairs possible. Before long, Kari was baking cookies for 4-H, planning snowmobile outings for the youth group, singing in the church choir, organizing bake sales, directing the children's Christmas program, and teaching children's Bible classes each week.

Marc was no less busy. Besides running the farm, he managed to fill his spare time with both Kari's church and community projects as well as his own.

Kari looked forward to Sheena's weekly letters, telling of her new job as a night janitor in a doctor's office complex, of her visits with Amanda, and of her weekly attendance at the neighborhood chapter of Alcoholic's Anonymous. When Marc suggested they send Sheena an Amtrak ticket to Wisconsin as a Christmas present, Kari's whirlwind of activities became a tornado. An old-fashioned Christmas, that's what we'll have, she decided, one like her mother had never experienced. Even the weather cooperated, turning the brown stubble fields into a glittering world of white.

Almost before the last piece of Thanksgiving's pumpkin pie disappeared from the refrigerator, the aroma of sugar cookies, Christmas stollen, and gingerbread greeted Marc when he returned from morning chores. The clink-clack cadence of the sewing machine treadle echoed long into the night as Kari tirelessly crafted felt Christmas stockings to hang over the fireplace and gifts for each family member.

"When in doubt, read the directions," Kari muttered one morning as she removed the sleeve of Mindy's bathrobe for the third time. "Three days before Christmas, and I still have to finish—" Suddenly the telephone interrupted her concentration. She ran to answer it.

"Gerard resi—, oops, I mean, Wynters' residence, Kari speaking."

"Kari." Her mother's voice sounded weak, almost unintelligible. "This is your mother."

Kari gripped the receiver tighter. "Mom? Are you all right?"

"Yes, yes, honey, I'm fine. Well, maybe not so fine." A raspy cough interrupted the woman's speech.

"You don't sound fine," Kari insisted. "What's wrong?"

"I hate to do this to you, baby, but I'm afraid I can't make the trip north after all." Sheena broke into a second fit of coughing. "I'm so sorry. I know how much you were looking forward to spending the holidays together. I was too."

Kari ran her fingers through her hair and swallowed the lump of disappointment forming in her throat. "Oh, Mama, it's OK. I understand. Should you be in the hospital or something?"

"No, I'll be fine."

After Kari questioned Sheena further on her symptoms and her medication, they ended their conversation.

"I don't want you to be alone on Christmas," Kari wailed.

"Maybe I can make the trip after the new year. I should be feeling better by then."

When Marc heard the news, he suggested they open gifts on Christmas Eve with his family and drive the 150 miles to Chicago on Christmas morning to be with Sheena.

Christmas Eve proved to be everything Kari had hoped for. Her eyes sparkled with delight as she watched each family member open and enjoy the carefully crafted gifts she'd labored over. With each gift, Marc glanced over at her and smiled. His face beamed with pride.

Later, the family traditions continued with Mom Wynters telling the Christmas story to the grandchildren. Then they gathered around the piano and sang carols. As the last notes of "Silent Night" faded away, the family members joined hands to form a circle while Dad Wynters prayed for each member of the family. The prayer ended with a round of kisses and hugs.

"Listen, you kids be careful, driving to Chicago tomorrow," Dad warned. "There's supposed to be a blizzard coming down from Canada."

Marc patted his dad on the shoulder. "We won't take any unnecessary chances."

Snappy, pelting snowflakes bit Kari's nose and cheeks as Marc helped her into the pickup truck. "Maybe we should drive the truck tomorrow, instead of the car," he suggested.

"The larger truck tires provide better traction."

They didn't speak during the ride home. Only the purr of the motor and the chunk-chunk of the tire chains broke the stillness. Kari closed her eyes. A pleasant smile teased the corners of her mouth as she absorbed the muffled silence of a Wisconsin snowstorm.

The storm continued throughout the night. When Marc left the house way before dawn to do the morning chores, Kari bustled about the kitchen.

"Cream of Wheat would surely taste good this morning," she mumbled to herself, idly switching on the radio as she passed by. "We'll need to take a good hot drink along with us. Where did I put the thermos bottle?"

"It's a bitter cold world out there today, in case you haven't noticed," the announcer drawled in his usual nasal baritone. "And Christmas or no Christmas, no one's goin' nowhere. So since we have no place to go, let's just 'Let It Snow' with Steve Lawrence and Edie Gorme."

"Speak for yourself, my friend," Kari muttered. "Oh, yeah, it's with the picnic basket in the hall closet."

She glanced out the window as she passed. Fresh snow had already obliterated Marc's footprints leading to the barn. "Hmm, it's really coming down out there." She turned toward the stove to answer the teakettle's insistent call.

At the sound of Marc stomping the snow off his heavy workboots, Kari ran to the door. "I have everything ready," she began. "I didn't know whether you'd want egg salad sandwiches or peanut butter and jelly, so I made . . ." The worried frown on his face made her pause. "What is it? What's the matter?"

"I've been listening to WMDS. They don't expect the storm to let up for another thirty-six hours. It's said to be the worst blizzard the Midwest has seen in fifty years." He shook his head before going on. "The state police just closed the Interstate."

Kari's shoulders sank. She bit her lip and took a deep breath. "I guess I already knew." Wrapping her arms tightly about herself, she walked into the living room. After deposing a protesting Swietzer from the platform rocker by the fireplace, she sat down. "Poor Mama, poor Mama . . . Christmas alone."

Marc yearned to reach out and comfort her, but the right words refused to come. Instead, he hurried upstairs to shower and change for breakfast.

Kari stared into the dying embers of the previous night's cozy fire. She reached into the large wicker basket on the hearth, removed two logs, and tossed them onto the gridiron. Sparks spiraled up the chimney. The grandfather clock at the foot of the stairs gonged five times. She glanced at her wristwatch. "Hmm, I guess I'd better wait a few hours before calling Mama and giving her the bad news."

They ate their breakfast in silence while the D.J. on the radio intermingled his merry chatter and weather updates with Bing Crosby's "I'll Be Home for Christmas" and Elvis Presley's "I'll Have a Blue Christmas Without You."

By 9:00 a.m., Kari placed her call to Sheena. "Mom? This is Kari. Mom? Are you all right?"

The voice on the other end slurred. "Sssure, honey. Whasss-upp?"

"I suppose you've already heard the weather report. The highways are closed. It's supposed to be the worst blizzard to hit in fifty years."

"Tha-s-s-s-o? Magin that."

"Mom? Are you sure you're OK?" Kari scowled, her jaw tightened. "Have you been drinking?"

"Why, of course, baby. 'Tis the season to be jolly."

Tears filled Kari's eyes; her empty stomach lurched sickeningly. "Mama, you promised. You know what that poison is doing to you."

"Look, don't sit up there in your icy castle and judge, ya' hear? You might live in a rose-covered cottage, with your silver-armored farmer boy, but the rest of us slobs don't have it so good. So don't get preachy with me!"

"I love you. Is that so bad?" Kari pleaded.

Sheena hesitated, then answered, her voice empty of emotion. "I-I-I'm sorry, baby. I'm sorry for everything." The line went dead.

Kari whirled about, her eyes wide with terror. "Marc, call Amanda. She's got to do something! My mother's killing herself, and I can't do a thing to stop her."

Chapter 5
A Time to Die

Kari slammed the dirty dishes into the dishwater. How many times she'd replayed this scene, she couldn't count. "Here I am again," she muttered, "standing at this same chipped sink, washing mismatched tumblers, stained with booze and who knows what else!" She swallowed hard, fighting back a wave of nausea. "Why, God, why? Mom was doing so well."

As the water pipes from the Sandozas' apartment upstairs clanked and rattled their morning complaints, Kari attacked the cooking stains on the stove top with renewed vigor. "It isn't fair! It just isn't fair!" A week ago, she'd never have guessed she'd be spending New Year's Eve alone, in her mother's apartment in Chicago. When Amanda called, telling them Sheena had been taken to Cook County Hospital and was listed in serious condition, Marc insisted Kari hurry to her mother's bedside.

"She needs you. After you assess the situation, I'll drive down if you need me." Knowing the added expense would strain the family budget, Kari balked, but Marc persisted. "She's your mother. You must go, regardless of the cost."

And now Kari felt alone, terribly alone. Amanda had offered to have Kari stay with her and the two children. But Kari refused. Now she questioned her decision.

Visiting her mother at the hospital shook Kari to her innermost core. Kari had never really believed that this horrid disease would win. The gaunt, wasted woman hooked up to a tangled web of tubes leading to faceless machines didn't begin to resemble the alive, vibrant woman her mother had become in the few short weeks in Wisconsin. A natural rosiness had returned to Sheena's cheeks. The shine was back in her overworked and overdyed hair. Rich whole milk, homemade bread, and wholesome vegetables had softened the hollows below her cheekbones.

The softening Kari saw happening inside her mother was even more dramatic. Without the numbing interference of alcohol, they'd become friends for the first time. Sheena had really seemed interested in getting her life together, physically and spiritually. She'd asked deep probing questions that had sent Kari and Marc scurrying to their Bibles and to their knees for the answers.

"Lord, what happened? What changed?" Kari slammed her fist on the countertop. "Her letters gave no warning."

Kari moved zombilike through the apartment, cleaning and straightening as she went. At the hospital, the staff allowed her to stay beyond visiting hours since it was obvious her mother was steadily weakening.

"Along with the jaundice and hepatic coma, your mother has suffered a GI hemorrhage caused by portal hypertension," Dr. Scott explained. "As you know, this leads to the development of collateral flow from the portal system to the systemic circulation."

"I understand, doctor," Kari assured her. "But what are her chances for recovery?"

The doctor's eyes mirrored Kari's concern. "The next forty-eight hours will be crucial."

Kari steadied herself against the corridor wall. "Dear God, not now," she breathed. "Give her another chance to find You."

The doctor grasped Kari's elbow. "Are you all right, Mrs. Wynters? Let me help you to the solarium."

Throughout the night Kari alternately paced and read the Gideon Bible she'd found on the Danish modern end table in the solarium. Fighting a wave of dizziness, she glanced down at her watch. She hadn't eaten in more than thirty-six hours. When the new shift came on duty, the night floor nurse insisted Kari go home and rest.

Reluctantly she returned to the empty apartment. Her first thought was to call Marc. She dialed, then hung up the phone after the first ring. "No, I'll wait until there's something to tell," she decided. "Right now, I need to eat something."

She wandered into the kitchen and opened the refrigerator. A baking soda box, a brown-jelled lettuce leaf, and some unidentifiable casserole concoction turned green were her choices. "I should have picked up something on the way home," she thought. She opened the bread box and found a stale heel of white bread. Shrugging, she dropped it into the toaster, then rummaged through the cupboard until she found an almost empty jar of peanut butter behind a half-filled bottle of red wine.

When the toast popped up, she scraped the peanut butter from the sides of the jar, spread it on the toast, and took a bite. Without warning, another wave of nausea surged through her. She tossed the bread into the sink and leaned against the counter. "Oh, no, not again," she wailed, swallowing frantically and gritting her teeth at the same time. "First, at home, at the hospital, now here."

She staggered into her old bedroom and fell, face down, onto the bed. Desperate to halt the room's wavelike action, Kari pressed the pillow into her face.

She remembered the wine in the cupboard. "Isn't wine good for indigestion?" When the pulsating rhythm in her head settled to a gentle moon-walk tempo, Kari inched her way back to the kitchen.

She removed the wine bottle from the cupboard and poured a small amount of its contents into a glass tumbler. As she sipped the red liquid, it warmed her throat, yet soothed her turbulent stomach. "I almost forgot what it tastes like," she mused, sighing with pleasure. "Ah, a little calmness around the edges to smooth out the rough spots."

Kari leaned back against the counter, cast her eyes toward the ceiling, and laughed. "How ironic, Lord, that my mother's demons would cure what ails me."

The image of her mother's jaundiced face swam before her eyes. How weak her mother had been to return to alcohol, knowing full well it would kill her. Kari shook her head in disgust. But then, Sheena had always been weak when either men or booze were involved.

Kari rubbed her forehead. A dull, nagging headache had replaced the dizziness and nausea. "If only I could just go to sleep and not wake up until this nightmare is over!" She grasped the translucent green bottle by the neck and poured herself a second round. "Maybe one more swallow will help me sleep."

Kari did sleep, but not the peaceful sleep she'd craved. Instead, nightmarish creatures blazoned through her slumber like starving rats set loose in a filled-to-overflowing grain bin. A frenzied Sheena screamed, "Don't call me mother," followed by the leering face of Keith, her mother's last live-in boyfriend. And one by one, each of Sheena's other love interests over the years paraded through her dreams, each laughing derisively at the weeping Kari.

The sound of her own sobs and the jangling telephone awakened the troubled woman. Shaking her head in an effort to clear the heavy fog of sleep and alcohol from her brain, Kari stumbled to answer it.

"Hello, yes, this is Kari Wynters. Yes—yes, I understand." She swayed uncertainly, closing her eyes against the inevitable. The receiver fell from her hand onto the floor beside the stand. "No—No—No—" She shook her head slowly back and forth at first, then increased the tempo to match the swelling volume of her cries until the entire apartment house echoed with her screams.

Before the first concerned neighbor knocked on the apartment door, Kari had collapsed onto the floor. She wrapped her arms tightly about herself as if to warm the cold emptiness she felt deep inside. "Why, God, why? It wasn't supposed to happen like this," she whimpered as she rocked back and forth in the middle of the living room. "Mom was supposed to find You first. Now, there's no hope. It's not fair!"

Slowly, through her hazy consciousness, Kari became aware of people surrounding her. Someone helped her to her feet. She moved about the crowded parlor in a daze. "Marc, I need you," she mumbled, fumbling for the telephone. When Kari misdialed her home number twice, Mrs. Dumont, the building superintendent's wife, dialed the number for her.

At the sound of Marc's concerned voice, Kari's tears came. With only her "Hello? Marc?" he understood and reached out to her, comforting, soothing, assuring.

Kari tried to string together a coherent message between her sobs.

"Don't worry, honey, I'll call Aunt Amanda to help you until I can get there," Marc encouraged, "I'll be there in three hours or less. Remember, I love you." The line went dead.

Kari composed herself long enough to assure the faceless crowd that she was fine. After closing the door on the last neighbor, she wandered about the apartment. Sheena was everywhere, yet nowhere.

She walked into her mother's bedroom and opened the closet door. Idly, she looked through the clothes inside. The polyester, leopard-print jumpsuit! Running her fingers along the smooth, silky sleeve, Kari remembered how she disliked the outfit on Sheena. She looked down at the floor. Her mother's five-inch-heel, rhinestone-studded, clear-plastic shoes had tipped over onto their sides. "And those ugly things—her 'let's party' shoes." Kari snorted.

"Cheap, cheap, cheap," she muttered, turning back toward the bedroom. An empty wine bottle protruded from under the unmade bed. Kari bent to retrieve it. She clutched the bottle in her hand and strode from the room. "Nothing but a wasted wino."

When she reached the kitchen, Kari's gaze rested on the glass tumbler she'd left on the counter and the uncorked bottle that matched the one still in her hand. A flood of color suffused her neck and face. "No!" She shouted at the chorus of devils cackling inside her head. "It's different with me. Sheena was weak. She allowed the stuff to destroy her. I would never . . ." Sickened by the doubts hounding her, she threw the empty bottle against the wall. "I hate you, Sheena! I hate you for destroying yourself like this!"

Suddenly, Kari felt tired—very, very, tired. She reached for the remaining bottle and poured the rest of the liquid into the tumbler.

She raised the glass toward the ceiling. "Cheers!" A hopeless cynicism numbed her pain as the liquid spread its warmth throughout her body. "Maybe Shelly was right. Maybe I am no better than my heritage. Maybe I am just a dirty little kid from the slums, destined to make the same stupid mistakes my mother made. And maybe, maybe I just don't care anymore."

Chapter 6
A Time to Be Born

Kari rolled over in bed and reached for one of her trusty saltine crackers. During the past month they'd been as necessary to her daily routine as toothpaste or deodorant. She smiled as she nibbled the corners off one cracker. "What a way to start the day." The sounds drifting up from the kitchen brought a moment of disquiet to her otherwise tranquil mood. "Poor Marc, having to fend for himself each morning," she thought.

"It won't last much longer, my darling," she whispered, "at least it hadn't better. I'm looking positively anorexic. Best diet I've ever been on."

She ran her free hand over her still unsettled stomach, grinned, and took a deep breath. A baby—her and Marc's baby. The thought triggered another happy smile.

When she returned to Wisconsin after Sheena's funeral and her nausea and dizziness didn't stop, Kari put two and two together and reluctantly made an appointment with Dr. Williams, their family physician. He confirmed her suspicions—she was healthy, normal, and five weeks pregnant. That was four weeks ago. "So how long can morning sickness last?" she wondered.

Even though they'd planned to wait a year or two before beginning their family, both she and Marc were delighted with the news. No one else was aware of what Kari mentally referred to as "her weak moment" in Chicago. She nursed an overwhelming load of guilt, along with a hefty dose of self-disgust. She now understood Eve's bitter knowledge of good and evil. The former innocence of her beautiful new religion seemed tainted, scarred, forever jaded.

Exhibiting an energy born of vengeance, she attacked her guilt, head-on. "So I fell on my face," she thought. "I can still prove to God, to Marc, to the Wynters' family, including Shelly, and, if necessary, to the entire world that Kari Elaine Gerard Wynters can be the best wife, and now, the best mother ever!"

"And, Mama dear," she nibbled further along the circumference of the cracker, her mood darkening, "while I know you can't hear me, I won't make the same mistakes you did. There's no room in my life for alcohol or any of your other weaknesses, for that matter!"

A flash of gray darted through the open doorway and leaped onto the bed. "Swietzer," she laughed, "you know you don't belong up here on the bed." Kari scooped the kitten into her arms and buried her face in his fur.

On cue, Swietzer purred and kneaded Kari's chest.

Kari lifted the cat's paws, taking with them the lacy bodice on her favorite nightgown. "Ouch, you crazy cat. If you want to stay up here, you'll need to keep your claws to yourself."

"Honey," Marc called from the foot of the stairs. "I don't want to bother you, but where did you put the carton of oatmeal? I can't find it anywhere."

"I'll be right down." Throwing the covers back, she gingerly sat up and slid her feet to the floor.

"So far, so good." Kari wrapped her yellow quilted robe about her and shuffled downstairs to Marc's rescue.

Toward the end of February, her morning sickness was replaced with a glow of well-being. Throughout the bitter winds of March, in spite of April's capricious moods, Kari felt invincible. The life growing within infused her with energy and confidence. She never tired. She took to new tasks and responsibilities like a junkie to the needle.

Marc alternately marveled and worried over her frenzy of activity. When Mom Wynters cautioned her about getting overtired, Kari smiled yet continued her brutal schedule.

One evening after supper, Marc glanced up from the farm ledger sheets. "I don't know how some of our neighbors are making it financially this year. If I didn't pull in a few dollars here and there as a vet, we would be in deep trouble."

"Is it that bad?" Kari glanced around the corner from the kitchen, where she'd decided while putting away the supper dishes that the cupboards needed cleaning. "I could always go back to my nursing, work part time or something."

Marc shook his head. "You have enough to do right now."

"If everyone paid you for your veterinary services, we wouldn't have any financial difficulties," Kari called from the kitchen.

Marc sighed. They'd had this discussion before. "I talked with Jack Barron. They had a tight year last year. He's afraid they might not get their loan renewed."

"Surely Mr. Morton wouldn't foreclose because of one bad year."

"No, not for one year. But for three, I don't know." Marc shook his head again and returned to his figures.

Kari removed the last of the spices from the cupboard by the stove. "Mr. Morton seems like such a nice man."

"It's not the bank manager's fault we've been on the verge of a drought for so long. He's just doing what his depositors hired him to do." Marc leaned back in his desk chair and stretched. "Well, it's about time for worship. I need to get as much sleep as possible. The Goodwins' prized Arabian is threatening to foal anytime, maybe tonight."

"Well, good!" Kari added emphatically. "The Goodwins certainly have enough money to pay their bills."

"Appearances aren't everything. They're mortgaged up to the hilt, just like the rest of us. Can you take a break soon so we can have worship together? I'm really beat."

"Why does he always decide to have family worship just when I least want to stop what I'm doing?" She wondered, gritting her teeth. "I'll be there in a minute."

With the last can of nutmeg and baking soda back in place, Kari reluctantly closed the cupboard door and hurried into the living room. She plopped down on the sofa and automatically picked up her needles, yarn, and the lavender-and-blue afghan she'd been knitting.

Marc rose from the desk and strode across the room to join her on the couch. He reached for the well-worn Bible on the coffee table and opened it.

"So how was your day, honey?"

"Do you really want to know?" An edge of irritation seeped through her words. She dropped her hands to her lap. "First, I ruined an entire batch of bread this morning. I killed the yeast, I guess. Then, at the church ladies' weekly prayer luncheon, Mrs. Lipcott complained because her little Sarah wasn't allowed to join the Blue Birds—she's only five, you know." Kari warmed to her subject.

"The woman stared right at me as if I were the one who made the stupid age rules. Then, during the meal, all the women at my table had to retell their horror stories about having babies. I swear, if all their tales were true, fright would be the best birth-control method going."

Marc laughed.

"Oh, it's easy for you to laugh. You're not the one anticipating the ordeal," she snapped, returning her attention to her knitting. "Men!"

"I'm sorry, Kari," Marc soothed. "I wasn't trying to be insensitive to your fears. I was just laughing at your vehemence."

"Then laugh, I don't care," she sniffed. "Can we get on with this? I have to get back to work in the kitchen."

"Why don't you take a break for tonight? We could just sit here and cuddle in front of the fire for a while like we used to."

Kari jumped to her feet and threw the afghan and needles into her knitting basket. "See, there you go, expecting me to be romantic after making light of my very real anxieties."

"Hey! What's going on? Did I miss something here?"

Kari's lower lip quivered dangerously. "And then you aren't even sensitive enough to know what you did!"

Marc sighed. An all-too-familiar pattern was repeating itself. "Look, I'm sorry. Can we start over? I'll read a text for worship, have prayer, and call it a night, OK?"

"I hardly feel much like praying now!" Kari dropped onto the sofa like a petulant teenager recently denied telephone rights.

Marc flipped through the pages of his New International Bible, ignoring her last remark. "I'll start at Ecclesiastes 1:3. 'What does man gain from all his labor at which he toils under the sun? Generations come and generations go, but the earth remains forever. The sun rises and the sun—' "

"Marc," Kari whispered breathlessly. "Marc, I felt something. Here—right here." She grabbed his hand and placed it on her stomach. "The baby kicked. A real kick. Not just the butterfly flutter that I've felt before. There! Can you feel it?" Tears glistened in her eyes as she turned inquiringly toward him.

They both held their breath for a moment. When the next kick came, Marc's eyes filled with wonder and delight. "That's our baby. That's really our baby," Marc gasped. "Somehow, before this moment, this whole pregnancy thing didn't really seem real."

Kari sniffed back her tears. "It's real all right, but I know what you mean."

They sat for several minutes, his hand on her stomach and her hand on his, both hoping to experience again the sensation of new life. When it was obvious they'd have to wait for another time to enjoy the next performance, Marc drew Kari tenderly into his arms. "Please my love, take care of yourself and this precious life within you. I worry about you sometimes."

Kari snuggled down into his arms. "I know, but I just want to be the best wife you could possibly ever have."

He lifted a stray ebony curl from her cheek and placed it behind her ear. "You are all of that and more. Don't you ever think otherwise!"

Lines of strain and worry crossed her brow for a moment. "I wish I were," she mumbled into his chest. "I only wish I were."

In between committee meetings, youth outings, and home responsibilities, Kari had been reading about the effect of alcohol on unborn children. Having come from generations of alcoholics herself, she worried about the baby she carried. Guilt from her own actions while in Chicago caused her to swing first from a frenzied search for assurances from God to utter cynicism and despair.

"Marc," she began one evening as she sat by the fire, reading a book and Marc sat in the rocker, reading the newspaper, "have you considered that there could be something wrong with our baby?"

He dropped the paper onto the floor and rushed to her side. "What happened? Are you all right? Is something wrong?"

Kari laughed nervously. "No, no. Nothing's wrong. I was just referring to my rather notorious chain of alcoholic ancestors. They say that 80 percent or more of the birth defects comes from chemical abuse such as drinking."

"Oh, you scared me for a moment. I thought—I don't know what I thought." Marc released his pent-up breath.

"I'm serious, Marc."

"I know you are." He thought for a moment. "I guess we'd do what other parents in such circumstances do, we'd manage. With God's help, we'd manage. His promise to 'never leave nor forsake us' will have to be enough for now."

" 'With God's help,' there it was again," she thought. "But what if He forsakes us, like He did Sheena? What then," she wondered. " 'One day at a time,' if only I could return to that kind of innocence."

"Hey, enough gloom and doom." Marc sniffed in the direction of the kitchen. "How about a few of those peanut butter cookies you made today?"

"M-a-r-c . . ."

"But, honey, I'm just a growing boy," he teased, "and you're eating for two now."

Kari rose to her feet and cast him a baleful stare. "Wrong on both counts, but if you want to indulge, feel free. After all, you are an adult and can make your own choices, good or bad."

"Aw shucks." He grinned. "Talk about taking all the fun out of it! Then how about a vicious game of Scrabble before bedtime? No calories there, except the ones you burn off, trying to beat me."

"I'd love to but . . ." She glanced toward the open sewing machine in the corner.

"Forget that stuff. You get the dictionary, and I'll get the game—unless, of course, you're afraid you might lose or something," he challenged.

"Not on your life, Bozo." She grinned, shaking her finger in his face. "No Latin words allowed this time either."

Chapter 7

A Time to Build Up

Kari yanked a thorn from her index finger. "I hate weeds!" She surveyed the overgrown garden plot behind the house with disgust. Even after Marc tilled the ground with the tractor, stubborn weeds persisted, their roots burrowed deep in the sod. "Why was I so eager for winter to pass?"

A warm June breeze ruffled her soft shoulder-length curls. She sat back on her haunches for a moment, and without thought, massaged her slightly convexed abdomen. Laying her garden trowel aside, she rose to her feet and dusted off the knees of her jeans and the front of her calico print smock.

Swietzer, her constant companion, rolled back and forth in the newly turned soil, absorbing both the sun's rays and the earth's moisture. At the sound of her voice, he stopped and purred. "A trimester to go and I still have to walk with an arched back so people will even know I'm pregnant," she muttered impatiently to the life growing inside of her. "So when do you plan to become at least a bulge, little one?"

Kari shaded her eyes and looked out across the field behind the house. She smiled, warmed by the sight of her husband bouncing across a furrowed field on the tractor. Picking up her garden tools and the unopened seed packets, she rubbed her aching back, then returned to the house.

In spite of the hard work, she enjoyed life on the dairy farm. She loved the feel of the black, rich soil as she worked in the garden. She thrilled at the sight of green shoots, breaking ground. She felt sheepish about it, but she couldn't help the way her heart speeded up just to look out across the valley at the fields of hay and corn spread out before her like a plump, well-worn patchwork quilt. A border of Queen Anne's lace edged the fields, and all was domed by the endless blue sky.

With the arrival of July and August, community and church responsibilities dwindled in the little farming community in response to the frenzy of the growing season. The men worked in the hot, sultry fields from dawn to dusk while the women filled their days stocking their larders with fruit, vegetables, and preserves for the coming winter and their menfolk with hearty, nutritious meals.

With the supper dishes washed, Kari wandered out onto the front porch where Marc sat reading the newspaper. The squeaky spring on the screen door announced her arrival.

"My, it's hot," Kari said, picking up the portion of the newspaper Marc had laid beside the chair. She wandered over to the steps, sat down, and fanned her sweat-stained face with the local news section of the paper.

A warm, moist air mass had stalled over the central part of the state for weeks, causing the crops to flourish far beyond their usual abundance. The same warm, moist air mass kept the temperatures high long after the sun set each evening.

"That's the truth," Marc replied, barely glancing up from the financial page.

Kari tipped her head toward him. She loved the way his blond hair curled at the nape of his neck. Smile lines fanned out from his vibrant blue eyes; his skin was tanned and firm. Warm fuzzies filled her heart, successfully replacing her earlier exhaustion. The low backache that nagged throughout the afternoon was temporarily forgotten.

Restless, she stood and leaned against one of the white wooden porch posts. She gazed for some time, out across the field toward the river.

"I don't like the looks of those clouds," she said.

"Not much you can do about them," Marc mumbled.

"Your dad called it 'a mackerel sky' this afternoon. What's 'a mackerel sky'?"

Marc laid his paper aside and came to stand behind her. "A mackerel sky never leaves the ground dry." He placed his large, rough-textured hands gently on her shoulders and drew her close. "If you look at the clouds, you'll see they resemble fish scales. And that usually means rain."

"Just rain?"

Marc shook his head. "Clouds like that can bring tornadoes, hail, or just heavy showers—only God knows at this point. I'm hoping the storm will hold off a few more days 'till the crops are in."

Kari batted at a mosquito humming around her face. Marc captured her hand, planting a kiss on her fingers. "I guess I'll walk over to the barn. I want to check on the new heifer. She cut her leg today. Gotta' make sure it's not infected."

"Don't be too long," she called after him. "There's a serving of peach cobbler in the refrigerator with your name on it."

As Marc loped toward the barn, Kari ambled down the steps and across the lawn. A purple martin suddenly swooped down in front of her, catching his nightly meal of mosquitoes. "Go for it," she cheered. "One less pest to keep me awake tonight."

She watched as, one after another, lights came on across the valley—first, at the folks' place next door, then at the Barrons on the far side of the state highway. Idly, she massaged her rounded stomach and smiled the secret Mona Lisa smile of generations of mothers-to-be before her.

Thunder rumbled out of the sagging cloud cover. Its reverberations shook the earth beneath her. Startled, she flew toward the barn and Marc.

"Marc?" She paused at the stall where he knelt.

"Sounds like a real thunderboomer," he said, releasing the calf's hoof. He stood and walked the length of the barn's concrete corridor. "Better turn on the radio—see if there's a weather watch in the area."

Sure enough, the evening D.J. had interrupted his country/western discs to warn of severe thunderstorms across the center and southern portions of the state.

"Marc?" Kari inched closer.

"It's just a storm, honey," he soothed, turning off the radio. "Let's get back up to the house before the rain comes."

They stepped outside the barn as the first raindrops fell to the earth. The droplets exploded little hollows in the dust, sending up a steamy smell peculiar to rain on a hot night.

Before Kari and Marc reached the front porch, the rain pelted in earnest from the dark, churning sky. Jagged streaks of lightning rent the clouds, illuminating the path as they broke into a run. Marc bounded up the front steps, hauling a gasping and breathless Kari by the hand.

Within minutes, the seriousness of the storm became evident. From behind the protection of the screen door, Marc stared out, his face drawn and gray. Kari ached for him. They were his fields ready to harvest. He had invested hours, sowing, cultivating, and, yes, even loving the crops to perfection. And there was absolutely nothing he could do now but wait. A flash of lightning lit up the yard; thunder crashed, but she hardly heard it. Maybe it won't be so bad, she told herself, casting a nervous glance toward her husband. Maybe it won't damage the crop.

When the first hailstones fell, Marc's shoulders sagged in defeat. Kari took one of his tightly clenched fists into her hands and kissed each of his rough, calloused fingers. "It's OK, honey. It's OK."

But she knew it was far from OK. She knew the hail would cut wide swaths through the fields, smashing hay to the ground, toppling corn, wheat, and any other crop in its path. Tears welled up in her eyes as she thought of how the hail would pound and beat the plants, utterly destroying months of hard work.

"Let's go to bed, Marc," she suggested. "There's nothing you can do 'till morning."

Marc allowed himself to be led up the stairs. A heavy stillness settled about the couple as silently they held each other in the darkness. The rain and hail drummed relentlessly on the roof over their heads.

Long after Marc had fallen asleep, Kari still lay awake listening—listening to the muffled drums at a military funeral. She rolled over, searching for a comfortable position in which to finally fall asleep, but without success. Her backache throbbed intermittently. Thankful that the baby inside had quieted down, Kari glanced at the clock on the nightstand. The illuminated dial read 2:35 a.m.

"It's no use," she groaned, throwing the covers back. She stepped into her slippers and padded toward the bedroom door. A sharp jab in her abdomen forced her to stop and catch her breath. She grasped the doorjamb to steady herself.

"False labor," she muttered as she stepped out into the hall, closing the bedroom door behind her. The doctor had prepared her for this eventuality. " 'Slight discomfort'—Dr. Williams and his euphemisms for agony. Two more weeks of this?"

She made her way down the stairs to the kitchen. "Time to frost my hair," she thought, opening the refrigerator door for a general tour of inspection. On the center shelf, the untouched peach cobbler beckoned her. A twinge of guilt momentarily stopped her.

"I'll eat just two meals tomorrow," she rationalized. Within minutes, the tiny piece she'd promised herself had become a third of the cobbler with an equal amount of vanilla ice cream piled on top. She savored each cold, sugary mouthful.

After rinsing her dishes in the sink, she curled up on the couch. Another pain gripped her. "Great, now I have indigestion," she thought. "Well, it serves me right, making such a pig of myself. Bet I won't get a wink of sleep tonight."

Flicking on the lamp beside the sofa, she picked up the current issue of a parenting magazine, then cast it aside. Restless, she strode over to the bookcase by Marc's desk and chose a book to read. But the book didn't hold her attention any better than the magazine. As the hours passed, her stomach relentlessly gurgled, churning away at the peach cobbler and vanilla ice cream. She curled up on the couch again, hugging a throw pillow to her stomach and wallowing in her misery.

Before the pink crescent heralding a new day lighted the horizon, Kari heard Marc tiptoeing down the stairs and out to the kitchen.

She snapped awake. "Marc?"

"I'm sorry," he whispered. "You were sleeping so peacefully, I didn't want to waken you."

"Isn't it a bit early to start the morning chores?" She asked, peering over the back of the sofa at Marc.

His eyes were puffy with blue half-moon shadows beneath them. He rubbed his whisker-stubbled cheek. "I thought I'd

go out and have a look at the fields before I start the milk-
ing."

"May I go with you?"

Marc stopped a moment, as if to say, "I'd rather be alone,"
then reconsidered. "I guess so."

"I'll run upstairs and throw on some clothes. It won't take
me a minute." She dashed for the stairwell, but doubled over
in pain on the first step. "Oof," she groaned.

"Kari!" Marc ran to her side. "What's wrong?"

She winced and gasped, "Nothing I don't deserve. I have
indigestion from making a pig of myself on peach cobbler and
ice cream."

"Are you sure?" he insisted.

"I'm fine now," she reassured him. "I'll be right down."

Marc was waiting in the pickup when Kari reappeared.
Regardless of his haste to assess the crop damage, he drove
over the bumpy farm road at a slow, controlled pace. The
truck fishtailed back and forth on the mud-slick surface. At
the top of the hill, he stopped the truck and climbed out.

All around them, crops lay battered and broken. In low
spots the water lay in shiny metallic puddles. Even the
black-eyed Susans along the road lay mushy, trampled by
the force of the wind, rain, and hail.

As Kari climbed from the cab, a pain sharper than any of
the previous pains stopped her. She doubled over, forcing
herself to breathe in short pants. That was what all pregnant
women were told to do. Of course that was during labor, not
during an attack of indigestion. She glanced at her watch. It
had only been five minutes since her last cramp.

"Five minutes?" Warning bells clanged. Her nurse's training suddenly cut in. She frowned. "This couldn't be—no, it's
two weeks until my due date."

While she sat arguing with herself, Marc disappeared over
the crest of the hill. Kari stared at the hands of her watch as
they inched, second by second, toward the next number. Exactly five minutes later, her stomach knotted into another
cramp. She groaned.

"Marc! Where are you?" Glancing out at the empty field,
she leaned on the horn, sending one long, continual blast out
across the fields.

The contraction had ended by the time a terrified Marc came into view. Yanking open the truck door, he gasped, "What's the matter? Are you all right?"

"I'm just fine, dear," she answered, calmly calculating the minutes until she could expect her next contraction. "I think you'd better drive me to the hospital. This baby just might be coming a tad early."

Panic swept across Marc's face. "Now?"

"Now! Unless you want to deliver your firstborn out here in the hayfield."

Marc leaped into the truck and slammed the door. "How far apart are your contractions?"

"About five minutes." Kari gripped the door handle and breathed a series of short breaths as another contraction began. "I take that back. Make that four minutes and fifteen seconds."

"Four minutes?" Marc screeched, his voice rising an octave higher than normal. He pressed the accelerator to the floor. The truck lurched forward, tossing Kari back against the headrest. She closed her eyes and groaned.

The countryside flashed by in the disjointed frames of a silent movie. The dotted line in the center of the highway rolled beneath them at an amazing speed. In record time, the outskirts of Beaver Dam came into view.

"I'm so sorry, Marc. Of all times to go into labor—right after we lose everything in a storm."

Marc reached across the seat and patted her hand. "Don't worry about that now! We have each other. That's more important than any hayfield or farm mortgage."

Another contraction, much closer than the last, interrupted her reply. "Hurry, Marc. Hurry!"

Simultaneously, Marc jammed his foot down on the accelerator. Before Kari's latest contraction had ended, the truck careened to a stop in front of the hospital's emergency entrance.

Chapter 8

A Time to Tear Down

"Sleep little baby, don't say a word. Mama's gonna' buy you a mockingbird. If that mockingbird . . ." The young mother crooned to the sleeping baby snuggled in the crook of her arm. The only other sound breaking the stillness of the chilly autumn night was the steady tick from the grandfather clock by the stairs.

She glanced about the darkened living room. How familiar this late night scene had become during the three months since Casey had arrived. Kari rested her head against the back of the rocking chair and closed her eyes.

Thanksgiving activities had left her exhausted. From somewhere, she knew she'd have to find enough energy for the Christmas season—Casey's first. The troubles of the day washed over her, leaving a profound tiredness. "And in a few hours it will all begin again," she mused.

"It isn't the work. Caring for my infant daughter, the 2:00 a.m. feedings, even the midnight bouts with cholic haven't been that bad," she admitted to herself. The hard part was having Marc gone so much of the time.

She missed the free time they'd had working and playing together. Kari assumed as many of the farm chores as was possible along with the care of the new baby. With the crop loss, it had been necessary for him to take an extra job, working with Mr. Savage, a housing contractor in Beaver Dam—this in addition to the farm chores and the occasional call for his veterinary skills. At least the contracting provided a steady paycheck.

Most of the time, Marc lacked the energy to converse

49

across the supper table or play a game of Scrabble. He barely had enough energy left at the end of the day to share the
day-by-day changes happening in their infant daughter's life.

Silently Kari stood up. The baby stirred in her arms,
Casey's lower lip puckered as if she were dreaming of meal-
time.

"Sh, little one," Kari whispered as she tiptoed up the
stairs. A clown nightlight illuminated the colorfully decorated
nursery enough for Kari to lower Casey into the ruffled bas-
sinet. With a fuzzy pink blanket tucked securely around the
sleeping child, Kari bent over and placed another kiss on
Casey's cheek. "You are so precious, my little one," she
whispered. The baby stirred; her tiny fist made its way to her
mouth.

Kari tiptoed from the room and closed the door. The clock
gonged four times. If I go to bed now, I'll interrupt Marc's last
half hour of sleep, she thought. Maybe I'll surprise him and
fix him an extra special breakfast this morning.

She tiptoed back down to the kitchen and flipped on the
light switch. Within minutes the aroma of baking biscuits
and scrambled eggs filled the house.

As she stood before the stove stirring the homestyle gravy,
Swietzer rubbed against her leg. "OK, OK, I get the message.
You want to go out." She opened the back door. A brisk cool
wind whipped her robe about her legs. "I am so tired. I sure
hope Casey sleeps most of the morning, after being awake so
long last—"

A twinge of guilt stopped her complaint midsentence. "Stop
complaining," she ordered. "Be thankful Mr. Savage took
Marc on. We could be in the same boat as the Barrons or the
Hastings family, facing possible bankruptcy. Somehow—"
She attacked the thickening gravy with a violence born of
frustration. "Somehow it doesn't seem fair—all that work and
for what?"

"Who says life is fair?" The voice behind her startled her
from her thoughts.

"Marc! I didn't hear you come downstairs."

"Probably not, you were so busy chewing out that pan of
gravy that a marching band could have paraded through the
parlor and you would have missed it."

Kari set the pan on a back burner and melted into Marc's arms. "I am sorry. It's just that I miss you so much."

"Hey," he teased, massaging her back as he held her close, "that's a left-handed compliment, I think—to be sorry that you miss me."

"You know what I mean. I feel so useless, staying here at home with Casey while you hold down two and sometimes three jobs to support us."

"You're doing more than enough. If I didn't have you and Casey to come home to, none of this would be worth it."

Kari slipped from his arms and padded across the room to the dish cupboard. "Regardless, I still think I should go back to work at the hospital, if only part time. It would really help our financial picture."

She could feel Marc's tension as he pulled a chair from the kitchen table and sat down. "We've already discussed this."

"No, we haven't. You've talked and you've decreed!" Kari slammed a plate onto the placemat before him, then returned to the kitchen counter. "Yesterday I talked with the nursing supervisor, and she's eager to hire me on evening shift, three-to-eleven, four nights a week—Thursday through Sunday."

"Kari—"

She held up her hand. "Not right away. By January, Casey will be weaned, so that will be one less concern. And Mindy and your mom have agreed to help with Casey whenever they're needed."

Marc jammed his fist against the table. The empty plate jumped in response. "I want my child's mother, not her grandmother or her aunt, to see Casey's first steps or hear her first words."

Kari nibbled uncertainly on her lower lip. "Well, don't you think I want that also?"

Marc looked up at his wife and shook his head. "I don't know what you want, but I do know you. You are an all-or-nothing person—for example, your church work, the community blood drive. The list goes on and on. You work yourself to a frazzle, leaving no energy for Casey."

"Oh?" Kari arched her left eyebrow. "And in that area, you are a paragon of restraint, I suppose?"

A heavy silence accompanied the rest of the meal. When they finished eating, Kari watched Marc leave the house, knowing their discussion was far from resolved.

She stormed about the kitchen, clearing the breakfast dishes. "He doesn't think I can handle it. He has no faith in me. Well I can—and I will!"

December flew by with its flurry of parties, pageants, and family traditions. A cold front swept down from Canada, depositing a heavy mantle of snow on the holiday festivities. However the cold front that settled within the gaily decorated walls of their home had a different effect on holiday spirits. As if by common consent, Kari and Marc refrained from bringing up the subject of Kari's returning to work again.

Silently, persistently, Kari worked toward her goal. If Marc noticed, he said nothing. Before the middle of January, Casey had happily adjusted to a bottle, and the hospital was prepared for Kari to begin working.

The night before she was scheduled to begin working, Kari knew she could no longer avoid the dreaded confrontation. Marc had just stepped out of the shower. She paused at the door of the bathroom, watching as he dried off and slipped into his yellow terry-cloth robe. His moist, tousled hair stripped five years from him. A smile teased the corners of her mouth. She longed to reach up and smooth the stray lock back into place. Instead, she took a deep breath.

"I start work at the hospital tomorrow afternoon."

Marc rubbed his chin. "You're going through with your plan, regardless of how I feel?"

"Yes." Kari nodded. "This is something I have to do for me as well as for the family finances."

Marc draped the wet towel over the towel rod. "Oh? Did you decide it was something you had to do before or after I objected?"

"Does it matter?"

"Perhaps."

"Are you saying I'm returning to my profession out of spite or stubbornness?"

He didn't answer.

"Well?"

Marc brushed past her and disappeared across the hall

into their bedroom. She followed. "Well?"

He removed his robe and threw it on the chair by the window. "Well what?"

"Is that all you have to say?" The knot in her stomach tightened.

"What else can I say? You know how I feel." Marc knelt beside the bed for a short time, then climbed silently into the bed. The room darkened as he turned off the lamp beside the bed.

Kari dropped to her knees on her side of the bed, mumbling beneath her breath, "The lord of the manor has decreed, so his faithful subject must acquiesce." After reciting a rote prayer, she arose and slipped beneath the bedcovers.

In the darkness, Kari mentally traced her fingers over the quilt's interlocking pattern. Even the black, moonless night couldn't hide the unhealthy tension permeating the room. A part of her longed to reach out and massage the tension from her husband's shoulders and back. Another part of her knew that such a touch would imply weakening on her part. "How," she wondered, "can I love him so much, yet harbor such strong feelings of anger at the same time?"

"It's the right thing to do," she argued. "We desperately need the money. Am I wrong," she asked herself, "to insist on doing this?" In the isolation of the night, Kari had to admit to herself, that while she felt an overwhelming sadness at the chasm between them and at the hours she would be separated from her baby, she also eagerly looked forward to the opportunity to practice her medical skills again. "Why must everything in life be a win/lose situation," she wondered, "even when choosing between two good things? If only Marc would be more reasonable." With a forced determination, she turned away from her husband, her face resolutely to the wall.

Chapter 9

A Time for Broken Vows

The elevator doors closed behind the last guest leaving third floor east. Kari sighed and reached for her stethoscope. "Now," she thought, "to get all of the patients settled for the night." She dreaded the long drive home on the icy roads. And from the reports she'd heard throughout visiting hours, the least she'd battle would be slick road surfaces. Occasionally, bad weather had forced Kari to stay in town for the night with her friend and nurse's aide, Bitsy Harper.

The blond, scatterbrained Bitsy met her as Kari came out of Room 312. "Mr. Evans, in Room 317, wants something for pain."

"I'll check on him right away." Kari smiled. "Dear Mr. Evans, all he really ever wants is a little TLC," she thought. "Don't we all?"

Kari completed her round of temperature taking, blood pressure checks, and pulse readings, being certain to take a little extra time with Mr. Evans. After handing out the night medications, she returned to the nurse's station.

"Have you looked outside recently?" Bitsy inquired. "What a snowstorm—even for Wisconsin! We'll be lucky if our replacements arrive on time for the next shift. I bet you don't get home tonight."

"Oh," Kari sighed, "I hope you're wrong. I've so much to do tomorrow. Casey has her monthly physical, and Marc asked me to—"

"Tell it to our freaky weather. Snow in April!" Bitsy tipped her head toward the large plate-glass window across the hall in the solarium. "I plan to stop at the Dew Drop on the way home, have a few drinks, then head home. Want to come along?"

Kari shook her head and smiled. "I just need a comfortable place to sleep. I should give Marc a call though, so he won't worry."

"You have a key to the apartment. Help yourself to the guest room. I'll be in sometime after midnight—if any of the bars in town are still open by the time we get off work, that is."

Kari nodded and dialed her home phone number. She knew Marc would agree; Marc would understand. He always did. But she knew, below the surface, the subzero tensions of the last few months hadn't eased for either of them.

The conversation was short, predictable, and unsatisfying. So many barriers—so many unspoken emotions between them. After she returned the receiver to its cradle, Kari stared down the darkened corridor. How long had it been since the two of them had spent time talking about something other than the baby, the farm, her job, or the finances. She ached for the long evenings of summer when they'd stroll hand-in-hand together along the boundaries of their property. "Will we ever find such peace and unity again?" she mused. The persistent blink of a patient's light on the electronic board broke through her thoughts. She hurried to answer the call.

Kari glanced in surprise at her watch when the night crew stepped off the elevator. Eleven fifteen—she'd been so busy, she hadn't realized the passing of time.

"Sorry we're late," Suzanne, the floor nurse began. "Have you seen the conditions out there? I finally had to park my car a few blocks from here and walk the rest of the way to work."

"I suppose the road crews will have it all cleared before morning," the night aide added.

"Not if it continues coming down as heavy as it is right now," Suzanne said. "Let's get on with reports so you gals can get out of here and get home tonight."

Within a few minutes, Kari and Bitsy stepped out into the blizzard. The crunch of the snow beneath their feet sent shivers up and down Kari's spine. "Will spring ever come?" she wondered.

"Leave your car parked in the lot. I'll walk with you as far as the bar," Bitsy volunteered. "Kevin is supposed to meet me there." Within a few minutes, they stood beneath the flashing red-and-yellow neon signs advertising Milwaukee's famous draft beers. "Are you sure you won't stay for a drink?"

"No," Kari replied, glancing toward the bar's warm, inviting interior. Memories of Kari's teenage years, illegally bar hopping with Sheena, flashed temptingly through her mind. The familiar strains of the hottest new country-western singer's rendition of "Have I Told You Lately That I Love You?" drifted out to the sidewalk where Kari stood. Suddenly she felt lonely, bereft of all security. She hesitated, then turned away.

"No, I really am too tired tonight, but you go ahead and have a good time, ya' hear?"

"Have it your way," Bitsy called as she stepped inside the building. "See you in the morning, hon."

Kari burrowed deeper into the woolen scarf about her neck and set her face into the pelting snow. The phone was jangling when she stepped into Bitsy's apartment. She ran to answer it.

"Hello?"

"Kari? This is Marc. Where have you been?"

Kari frowned. "Checking up on me?"

A silence followed. "Is that what you think?"

"I-I-I don't know. I guess not."

"I just wanted to catch you before you got to sleep to let you know the roads will remain closed most of tomorrow, so you might as well stay where you are."

"Oh, I'm sorry. I'm a little snappish tonight, I guess."

"Yes. Well, Casey sends her love," Marc added.

"And you?"

"I'll see you tomorrow night, OK?"

"Yeah. Right." The line went dead in her hand.

As Kari wandered through the empty apartment, she turned on each light, trying to ease the loneliness she felt inside. She hugged herself against an inner chill that defied the cozy warmth of the apartment. "It's too quiet. I need some noise," she decided, flipping on the television's remote control.

Johnny Carson's sardonic humor filled the empty living room. Kari changed the channel to a rerun of the seventies

TV hit "Little House on the Prairie."

"Hmmph," she snorted, "if only life were that simple. All our problems resolved in sixty minutes, minus commercials." Kari wandered over to Bitsy's well-stocked bar in the corner of the parlor. "Ginger ale, no ginger ale," she muttered. Her eyes rested on the line of sparkling bottles before her.

She paused, turned to walk away, then remembered the unsettling phone conversation. Defiantly, she grabbed a glass from the mirrored shelves and an already opened bottle of gin. Before she could change her mind, Kari poured the liquid into the glass and drank it. "So there, Marc Wynters!"

Clutching the bottle in one hand and the empty glass in the other, she returned to the sofa and tried to concentrate on the television program in progress. Another drink, and the theme song for the late night movie was playing.

Kari jumped at the sound of a key in the front-door lock. An empty liquor bottle clattered against the edge of the coffee table, falling to the floor. "That can't be Bitsy. She won't be home for hours," she argued.

"Well, hello, you still awake?" Bitsy inquired. "I thought you'd be asleep long ago. What time is it, anyway?"

"I really don't know," Kari admitted. "I got watching this TV program and—" The two women glanced toward the TV screen. The end of programming pattern blazed across the screen. "Oops," Kari giggled.

Bitsy's gaze traveled from the empty bottle to Kari's flushed face. "Why, you little devil you," Bitsy laughed. "You're smashed."

Kari tried to shake her head, but her unaccustomed dizziness prevented any such action. "I'm so embarrassed."

"Hey, don't be." Bitsy removed her coat and hung it in the closet. "I always said you should loosen up a bit. But boy, I must admit, when you loosen, lady, you really loosen. Here, let me help you to your bedroom."

Kari giggled. "The blind leading the blind, huh?"

"More like the drunk leading the drunk, I'd say."

Kari stopped short and tried to focus her gaze on Bitsy's face. "I'm not drunk!" Kari snapped.

Bitsy laughed. "Well, you could'a fooled me."

The next day Kari slept, oblivious to the snowstorm outside. It was late afternoon when Bitsy shook her awake.

"The phone," Bitsy mumbled. "It's your husband."

"Oh." Kari rolled over and tried to sit up. Her head pounded to the unrelenting rhythm of a jackhammer; her tongue tasted as if a regiment of wart hogs had stampeded across her taste buds. "What time is it?"

Bitsy squinted at the wall clock. "About noon."

Kari staggered to the telephone.

"Kari?"

"Yes," she drawled, "what is it?"

"Casey had a fever last night."

Kari tried to focus her attention. "What? Is she all right?"

"Yes, Mom came over and helped."

"I should have been there!" She said, her voice revealing her sudden guilt.

"Uh, yes. Well—anyway, we used up the baby aspirin," Marc added. "If you could stop and get some on your way home tonight—"

"Sure, I'll pick up a bottle."

"Are you all right? Your voice sounds kind of strange."

"I'm fine, Marc," Kari insisted. "Was there anything else we might need over the weekend?"

"No, I don't think so."

Kari cradled the receiver against her neck and pushed her disheveled hair from her face. "Are the roads cleared yet?"

"The road crews should have everything under control by tonight."

"Great!" Kari paused. "Then I'll see you tonight. Hug Casey for me."

"Right. Sure." Marc's voice held a strange quiver. "See you then. Take care."

Kari hung up and staggered into the bathroom. In the shower, she fought to scrub away her feelings of guilt and remorse. What had gotten into her—boozing it up like that? "Why, you're no better than your drunk of a mother," she scolded, as the shower spray mingled with the tears sliding down her cheeks.

Kari emerged from the bathroom to find Bitsy at the kitchen table, a partially filled glass in her hand. Kari glanced at the amber-colored bottle in the center of the table.

"Isn't it a little early for that stuff?"

Bitsy blushed. "It's the only way I can get going the day after a night on the town."

As she walked over to the cupboard and removed a bowl from the shelf, Kari sighed. How many times over the years had she heard Sheena say the same thing? "I will never let myself fall into a trap like that," she vowed. "And, last night will never be repeated!"

Chapter 10
A Time to Weep

Kari slammed her foot down on the gas pedal, hoping to out-run the burning ache in the pit of her stomach. While the world around her had burst forth overnight with signs of spring, her heart still shivered from the bitter winds of winter.

"Why?" She shouted to the empty seat beside her. "Why must every discussion with Marc end in a fight? Why can't we just sit down and talk things out reasonably? And he wonders why I dread coming home from the hospital!"

The prolonged snowstorms had necessitated her staying over at Bitsy's apartment more often than Kari ever imagined. The stress between Kari and Marc increased in direct proportion with her home absences. Then Kari made additional excuses to avoid returning home at the end of her shift. By springtime, she managed to stay in town once or twice every weekend she worked. While she prided herself in not bar hopping with Bitsy and her friends, Kari would return to the empty apartment and "have a few" to ease her stress. Occasionally, after a rough shift at the hospital and even rougher conversation on the telephone with Marc, she had more than a few.

It was in this state that Bitsy came home and found Kari one morning. Without a word, Bitsy reached down and pick-ed up the empty liquor bottle and carried it into the kitchen.

Kari mumbled something about needing a shower and stumbled into the bathroom. When she emerged from her shower, Bitsy confronted her. "Kari, if you're going to drink so much, I would appreciate it if you would contribute to the supply."

"Why, I—I didn't know the little bit of alcohol I might use bothered you," Kari retorted defensively.

"Little bit?" Bitsy held up the empty bottle in her hand. "Hey, I don't mind your staying here with me. In fact, I enjoy it. But, I just can't afford to support your habit."

"My habit?" Kari's eyes snapped with anger. "I'm not the one who goes out and hits every sleeze joint from here to Madison almost every night."

Bitsy held up her hands, signaling a timeout. "Wait a minute. I'm not your enemy. I love you like a sister."

"Well," Kari huffed, "you have a funny way of showing it."

Bitsy stopped and stared at her distraught friend, then set the bottle down on the table. "Yeah, you're right. I haven't been much of a friend, have I? Sit down, dear friend; it's time we had a talk."

Bitsy's voice echoed and reechoed through Kari's brain. Grabbing for her head, Kari shrieked, "Stop yelling! Ooh, Bitsy," she then whispered, "stop yelling."

"When I first met you," Bitsy began, "I thought you had to be the luckiest woman in the world. You had a darling baby, a hunk of a husband who really loved you, a new job at the hospital. But even more than that, I sensed something within you, something spiritual that I would have given my right arm for. Maybe—maybe I hoped whatever it was might rub off or something. Dumb, huh?" Bitsy swallowed hard and grabbed for a tissue from the box sitting on the counter. "Anyway, you had it all."

"But I—" Kari interrupted.

"No, hear me out. If I stop now, I'll never have the guts to start again," Bitsy explained. "Over the last few months, I've watched you throw it all away for this stuff." She pointed to the bottles.

"Hey, get off my back, OK? I'll pay you for your precious booze, if that's what you want," Kari snarled. "Would you like me to count out the number of cornflakes I eat for breakfast?"

"Money isn't the issue here. Casey is, Marc is, and you are!"

"Well, excuse me." Kari lurched from the table, grabbed for her aching forehead, and swayed. Pulling herself together with as much dignity as her inebriated body would allow, she marched from the room.

Behind her she heard Bitsy mutter, "Oh boy, I really blew it this time."

Kari slammed the door to the bedroom behind her, then leaned against it for support. She glanced about anxiously, trying to focus her brain or at least her eyes on her surroundings.

"I gotta get out of here!" She threw her overnight case onto the bed and gathered what few of her belongings she could spot, then slammed the case shut. Without a word, she left the apartment, despite Bitsy's pleas. "Wait! You can't drive in that condition. Let me call you a cab."

"So call me a cab," she giggled in a sing-song tone. "I'm a cab. Kari's a cab." Maneuvering the flight of stairs to the street level proved to be trickier than she expected. They shifted beneath her feet like a demented escalator. She felt dizzy, lightheaded.

By the time she opened the apartment house door and stepped out onto the sidewalk, all she could think about was air—fresh, cool air. Outside, the world had become a swirling, stomach-lurching carnival, owned and operated by the devil himself. Kari made her way to the curb. Unable to proceed, she leaned against a parked car. She ducked her head, hoping not to be seen by people driving by. From past experience, she knew it was only a matter of time before she added public humiliation to her ever-growing list of frustrations.

Kari was too busy fighting her nausea to hear a pickup truck screech to a halt beside her. A tall, blond-haired teenage boy jumped from the cab and rushed to her side.

"Kari," Michael asked, "what's the matter? Are you all right?"

"I—I'm sick. I think I'm going to throw—" She failed to finish her sentence before she carried out her threat.

Michael ran for the truck and returned with a handful of tissues. "Do you have the flu or something?" After helping her clean up, Michael wrapped his arm about his sister-in-law's shoulders.

"Yes, yes." She swallowed hard. "That must be it. It must be the flu. What are you doing here?"

"I was on my way to the feed store for Dad when I saw you come out of Bitsy Harper's place," he explained. "I think I should take you home."

"But my car." Kari pointed in the general direction of the apartment house parking area.

"Don't worry. We can pick it up later." Without giving her a chance to object further, he led her to the truck.

As she opened the cab door, she squinted up into Michael's face. "You're a lot like your brother, Marc."

"Thank you." Kari noticed him suddenly draw away from her as he helped her into the truck, then slam the door.

Once he had settled himself behind the wheel, Michael glanced over at Kari. "Whew! You sure smell of liquor. Bitsy must have thrown some party last night. You might as well have come home last night for all the sleep you probably got." Kari reddened and stared out the side window to avoid his gaze.

Michael eased the truck into the late morning traffic toward home. Following his sudden move toward the dashboard, ear-splitting music blared from the radio. He made no move to lower the volume when Kari grabbed her head and covered her ears to block out the pain of the deafening noise.

"I'll be hanged before I ask him to turn that down," she muttered, glancing toward her brother-in-law from the corner of her eye. The set of his jaw told her Michael was no fool. He knew she'd been drinking and determined to make her pay for her sins.

"Sins! How like a Wynters!" Tears sprang up in her eyes. "That's not fair," she scolded herself. "But who said life was fair?"

Kari huddled next to the door as if willing herself invisible. At one time, she knew, she could do no wrong in Michael's eyes. At one time—but no longer. She felt a sharp pain in her heart. She'd tumbled from the precarious pedestal Michael had constructed for her. "Well," she silently argued, "I never asked for adulation from him or anyone else." Yet the pain remained.

The ten-mile ride home seemed both interminable and brief. Without a word, Michael stopped the truck in front of the farmhouse, hopped out, came around, and opened her door. Kari searched his eyes for a flicker of compassion. She found none.

Without a word, he helped her into the empty house. As he turned to leave, he said, "If you care, Casey is at our house. Marc had an emergency call at the Anderson spread this morning." Then he was gone.

Kari watched from the window over the kitchen sink as Michael's truck spun gravel the full length of the driveway. The tears she'd been fighting to control tumbled down her cheeks. A new wave of nausea flooded her. With a sob, she turned on the faucet and splashed cold water over her hot, tear-stained face. Will this be the end, she wondered, for Marc and me? Have I, indeed, lost everything, like Bitsy says?

"If I can just rest a while—sleep," she mumbled. "Yes, what I need is a little sleep." She was so tired. Tired of the tension and uncertainty. Tired of constant bickering. Tired of her own failures. Tired of living. Slumping to the cold kitchen floor, Kari sobbed until she no longer possessed the energy to draw a steady breath, until her throat was raw and aching. She drew her feet up under her and curled up into a fetal ball and fell asleep. Sunlight from the kitchen window cast a soft pool of light over Kari's tangled curls and cascaded onto her flushed, tear-stained face. It warmed, anesthetized, soothed her into a dreamless slumber.

She awoke to a gentle swaying motion. She could feel strong arms holding her, carrying her up the stairs. "Marc?" she slurred, her arms lifting automatically to encircle his neck.

"Go back to sleep. I'm just putting you to bed."

She snuggled her face into the opening of his shirt. "You know—you know everything, don't you?"

His arms tightened about her.

"I'm so sorry." She partially opened her eyes. Her heart wrenched at the pain she read in his eyes. "We need to talk."

"Sh," he replied, "not now—tonight." After placing her on the bed, he disappeared across the hall to the bathroom and returned with a moist face cloth and towel. Gently, he cleansed her face, neck, and hands, then helped her out of her soiled clothes and into a clean flannel nightgown.

"Don't worry about your shift at the hospital. I've already called and told them you're sick," he said as he eased her beneath the bedcovers. He hesitated for a moment as if wanting to say something more. But instead, he planted a kiss on her forehead and left the room, pulling the door quietly shut behind him.

Hours later, Kari awoke to the aroma of potatoes frying. In spite of the pain in her head, she smiled when from the bottom of the stairs, Marc clanged a metal spoon against one of her pots. "Wake up, sleepyhead. You have exactly seven minutes to shower and dress for dinner."

Even after the shower, Kari inched cautiously down the stairs and into the kitchen. The sides of her head painfully expanded and contracted to the slightest sound. Marc's back was to her as she slid into her place at the table.

"Casey will be spending the night with my folks," he explained, dishing out the simple meal he'd prepared. "I figured it might be easier to communicate if she weren't here to overhear us."

Instead of talking as they ate, they both found themselves reluctant to disturb the tenuous balance they'd achieved. When they finished eating and had washed the supper dishes, Marc reached out from habit to take her into his arms. He stopped, then drew back.

"I guess we can't put it off any longer, huh?" His steel blue eyes bore deep into hers. He took a deep breath and walked determinedly into the parlor.

She followed. After scooting the array of throw pillows into the center of the couch, they sat down, one at each end of the sofa. Kari gnawed on her lower lip while Marc studied the callouses on his hands.

Finally, he sighed through a clenched fist and spoke. "I saw Michael today."

"I know," Kari whispered.

"How long has this been going on—all winter?"

"For the most part," she admitted.

Marc shook his head angrily. "I won't lie to you. I'm hurt. I'm angry. I want to punch something or someone!" He slammed his fist into one of the throw pillows beside him. "I wish I could say I understand, but I don't."

"How could you?" she snarled, barely above a whisper. "You, a bona fide, card-carrying member of the righteous, upstanding Wynters family?"

He turned toward her, surprise showing on his face. "Do

you resent my family that much?"

Immediately she felt contrite. "No, no, it's not their fault. They've treated me better than I deserve." She paused to take a breath. "Look, this situation really isn't as bad as it looks. I got upset after we hung up last night and had a few too many drinks. I only drink to get through the hard times," Kari defended herself.

The gentle ticking of the hall clock replaced Kari's explanations. "If my occasional glass of wine or shot of whiskey bothers you that much, I'll stop, OK? It's not like I go out boozing every night with Bitsy and her friends."

Marc eyed her until Kari nervously looked away. "I can stop, you know. I know what you're thinking—that I'm a good for nothing drunk just like my mother!"

"I never thought that about her, and I certainly don't think it of you," he answered, his even, steady tone not completely belying his anger. "I love you, Kari. I would do anything for you, short of standing by and watching you destroy yourself." He clutched a small throw pillow in his hands until his knuckles drained of color. "Unfortunately, this is a problem only you can face. You need professional help."

"What?" Kari jumped to her feet.

"Hear me out—"

"No! No, I won't." She paced back and forth in front of the empty fireplace. "Can't you even try to understand? I only drink when the pressures become too much to handle—pressures, I might add, that are most often of your making."

Marc leaped to his feet, instantly planting himself directly in her path. "I am trying to be understanding about this, but I won't bear your guilt!" He grabbed her by the shoulders. "It is your choice and no one else's to face your problems through the bottom of a liquor bottle."

"Let me go!" she shouted. "You can't bully me, Marc Wynters."

In shock, he glanced down at his whitened knuckles and stepped back from her. He looked at his fingers as if for the first time, then ran them distractedly through his hair. He walked to the far side of the room.

"Somehow, I don't know you anymore." His gaze rested on his Bible lying on the lamp table where he'd left it earlier in the afternoon. He strode over to the table and picked it up. "When I first met you, you faced your problems with this. I can still hear you repeating Isaiah 40:31 as you climbed out of bed for Casey's 2:00 a.m. feedings. 'They that wait upon the Lord shall renew their strength. . . .' "

"Don't preach at me, Marc," she warned through clenched teeth.

"Is that the problem? Did I, did the entire family expect too much of you—more than you were capable of giving at the time?" Kari watched Marc sink into the chair, his Bible sliding, unnoticed, to the floor. "What has happened to us?"

Compassion tinged with sorrow swept momentarily through her, only to be replaced with the bitter memories of unfinished battles, unresolved anger, and unspoken accusations. "Look I am strong enough to handle my supposed drinking problem without you, or your family's, or even God's help. OK?" Kari's lips tightened into a thin, pale line. "Regardless of what your sister Shelly might think."

"Shelly?" Marc started at the apparent change in direction. "What does she have to do with anything?"

"It doesn't matter. You want a super wife? You'll get a super wife—minus the booze, OK?"

"I never said anything about wanting a super—"

"If you'll excuse me, I think I'll go upstairs to bed—on the daybed in Casey's room." She whirled about and headed for the stairs.

"Kari, we haven't resolved anything."

"Good night, Marc."

She climbed the stairs with as much force and determination as she could muster. Lingering just inside the open nursery door, she listened, hoping to hear Marc's tread on the steps. Instead, she heard him storm from the house, the door slamming behind him.

Minutes ticked by, then hours. Marc did not return. The first hues of dawn warmed the eastern sky when she finally gave up and fell asleep.

Chapter 11

A Time of War

Marc bent down and picked up a smooth, flat stone. Taking a step back, he skimmed the stone across the surface of Beaver Dam Lake.

"Tsk, tsk, tsk." Kari chuckled while rolling her own stone in one hand. "Only three skips. You're losing your touch. Let me show you how it's done."

"All right, smarty-pants!" he replied. "Give it your best shot."

Arching one eyebrow, she directed her attention first to the stone in her hand, then to the water. One mighty swing sent the stone skimming across the surface. One, two, three, four, five, six jumps.

Kari turned toward Marc, threw back her head, and laughed. "That's eight wins out of fifteen." Dipping her hand into the water, she splashed a handful at her startled husband. "Looks like I win for the day."

Hunching his back in a threatening stance, Marc lumbered toward her. The glint in his eye alerted her to his intent.

"Marc, Marc! You wouldn't dare!" Kari took off running down the beach.

"Oh, wouldn't I?" He set off in pursuit.

Wild ducks foraging the banks of the lake for food scraps scrambled in every direction as the young couple charged across the uneven lawn. Out of breath, Kari glanced over her shoulder just in time to be swooped off her feet and into Marc's arms.

"No! No," she squealed. "Put me down."

"Oh, don't worry, I'll put you down," her pursuer snorted, striding to the water's edge, "right where you belong."

"Really, Marc," she begged, "I don't have a change of clothes with me."

"You should have thought of that sooner," he threatened without breaking his stride. Sneakers and all, he entered the lake. Holding her away from his body, he dangled her over the water.

"If I go, you go too!" She grabbed for his neck.

"It will be worth it—" Only a startled cry from the grassy slope behind them halted the inevitable.

"Casey!" Kari pointed toward the blanket spread beside the unopened picnic basket. "Casey's crying."

Marc groaned. "Talk about crying on cue. How much did you pay her to do that?" Reluctantly, he lugged Kari to dry ground, and together they sprinted to the baby.

Kari bent down and lifted Casey into her arms. "Hi, sweetie. Oh ho, you need a change, huh?"

"I'll get the diaper bag out of the car," Marc volunteered.

A pleasurable warmth spread through Kari as she watched Marc cover the short distance to the parking lot. He walked with a confident, easy-going stride. Just like, she thought, when he left me standing in front of the railroad station in Columbus while he went to get his truck—so long ago.

She knelt down on the edge of the blanket. Casey whimpered as Kari laid her on the blanket and unpinned the soiled diaper. "Sh, Daddy will be right back, honey, and we'll get you all clean and dry again."

The previous three months had been good for Kari and Marc. Getting back into the swing of summer helped them both heal. With planting a garden, keeping house, caring for Casey, and maintaining her part-time job at the hospital, Kari had no difficulty keeping her promise to her husband that she would quit drinking. As for Marc, the further they got from their nightmare, the less concerned he seemed. Yes, she'd been right, she decided. She had no drinking problem.

Marc set the diaper bag on the blanket, then lay down on the grass beside Kari. The baby gurgled at the sight of her father. He leaned forward and tickled Casey's chin. When Kari completed changing Casey's diaper, Marc lifted the laughing baby high into the air above his head.

Kari watched the two for a moment, then looked toward the lake. The late-afternoon sunlight sparkled on the water's surface, creating a captivating vision of light and shadow. A comforting peace coursed through her body. She shifted, drawing her knees up under her chin.

"I'm glad you suggested we pack a picnic lunch and come out here today, Marc. It's just what I needed."

He rolled over, placing Casey on her stomach in the middle of the red-plaid blanket. "It has been good, hasn't it—playing together again? We haven't had much time for that lately."

"I enjoyed Pastor Keeler's sermon this morning too."

"I'm glad," Marc whispered, an unnaturally cautious note creeping into his voice. Kari knew how careful he'd been not to mention religion to her. "Taking this weekend off from the hospital to be together was a good idea too."

She shrugged.

Lost in their own thoughts, the couple stared at the lake for some time—until Casey informed them it was time for her afternoon meal. Marc removed a jar of baby food from the bag and opened it.

"It must have been lonely out here in the middle of winter," Kari mused aloud. During one of their more serious discussions regarding their troubled winter, Marc had told Kari about the drives he'd made to the lake.

"I felt close to you here. It's one place that held only good memories for me," he explained. "Even with five feet of snow on the ground, I would come out here in the pickup and stare at the snow-covered lake and have it out with God. I felt so alone. I felt like I had to hold the family together all by myself."

But now, on such a warm summer afternoon, with the quacking of ducks and singing insects in the distance, and Casey eating little spoonfuls of puréed peaches, winter seemed a lifetime away to Kari. She smiled over at her husband, then down at her daughter. "How precious these moments are," she thought. "A second chance, not everyone gets a second chance."

The day passed too quickly for both Kari and Marc. The

setting of the sun brought on the evening mosquito brigade, forcing the family to reluctantly head for their parked car. From the safety of their automobile, they watched the sun disappear and the lights of the town blink on.

"Over the sunset mountains," Kari breathed the melody to the old familiar hymn they'd sung just that morning, "heaven awaits for me."

"I'm not as far gone as you may think, Marc," she began.

"I never thought—"

She raised her hand to interrupt. "I'd like it if we could begin having family worship together again—just thought you'd want to know."

Marc raised his eyebrows.

"Aren't you going to say anything?"

He cleared his throat. "If you're sure that's what you want."

"I'm sure," she stated emphatically. "I've stood in the hall outside the nursery and listened to the little worship you conduct each evening for Casey. And, I've felt left out sometimes."

"You're the one who—"

She slid across the seat and snuggled close to his side. "So, I've changed my mind."

When she noticed the tears glistening in Marc's eyes, Kari reached up and caressed his cheek. "Well?"

Gathering her into his arms, Marc held her tightly to him. "Dear heavenly Father," he prayed, his voice filled with emotion. "Thank You so much for bringing my beautiful wife back to me. She's been gone so long from me."

They wept, talked, and wept some more, long into the night until Casey reminded them it was time for all good babies to be placed in their cribs. Content for the first time in months, Marc and Kari drove home.

In the weeks that followed, Kari and Marc acted like newlyweds. Stolen glances, happy grins exchanged on the sly, and sharing numerous little surprises added a new, exciting dimension to their relationship.

At the hospital, Kari had mended her fences also. She and Bitsy were again best of friends. While Kari tired of Bitsy's continued attempts to drag her to Alcoholics Anonymous meetings, she enjoyed Bitsy's sparkle and friendship.

"You're coming over to my place tonight, for Sondra Benson's wedding shower, aren't you?" Bitsy asked one Sunday evening. Kari hadn't been back to the apartment since the embarrassing confrontation.

"Sure am," she replied. "Wouldn't miss it for the world."

At the end of the evening shift, the nursing staff left en masse for Bitsy's apartment. White honeycombed paper bells dangled from the ceiling and light fixture in the parlor with streamers of white, pink, and yellow—the bride's colors—linking them together. A large punch bowl occupied the center of the two folding tables pushed together along the wall near the kitchen doorway. An ice ring of live flowers floated atop the sparkling beverage. Chairs of varying styles and shapes lined the walls, filling in any open spaces that might have been available. If the additional furniture didn't fill the room, the milling guests soon did.

"Can I help with anything?" Kari inquired of her friend.

"You can add the booze to the punch," Bitsy replied, as she placed a large platter of hors d'oeuvres on each side of the punch bowl.

"There! I think everything's under control now."

"Where's the guest of honor?" Kari asked.

"Oh, Ellie, from pediatrics, is bringing her. I haven't any idea what story she's telling to get Sondra here."

The party came alive with the arrival of the bride-to-be and her deceitful co-worker. Blaring music from the stereo competed with the loud chatter. Kari wondered how the tenants in the neighboring apartments were handling the noise.

She kept busy until the wee hours of the morning, helping Bitsy repeatedly fill the punch bowl and restock the platters. Whenever there was a break in the action, Kari helped herself to a little of the punch. It wasn't until a wave of dizziness caught her off guard that she realized she'd not only drunk more of the beverage than she intended, but she had done so on an empty stomach. "Oh no," she groaned. "What will I tell Marc?"

Ellie, who was standing beside her, leaned closer. "What was that, honey?"

Kari reddened. "Uh, nothing, just thinking out loud."

"Great party, huh?" the woman continued.

"Yeah, great party." Kari inched away from the woman and into the kitchen. She leaned her forehead against the refrigerator, her remorse wrestling with her nausea for attention. "How could I let this happen? I've broken my promise to Marc."

She squinted up at the clock on the wall, trying to focus on the position of the hands. "Oh, my goodness!" she gasped. "It's time for Marc to begin chores. I gotta get home to Casey!"

Kari rummaged through the pile of jackets heaped in the middle of Bitsy's bed until she found her sweater and purse. After making as coherent an excuse as possible to Bitsy and to Sondra, she bolted out the door and down the stairs to her waiting car.

Once behind the wheel, she struggled to put the key into the ignition. Warning bells sounded within her head. "I shouldn't be driving," she decided. "Marc will have to find out. I can't risk my life and possibly someone else's by driving in this condition." She returned to the apartment and reluctantly placed her call.

Half an hour later, Marc's truck pulled to a stop alongside the curb where Kari was waiting. She climbed in.

"I'm sorry, Marc," she began. "I don't know how it happened. Really. I guess I drank a little here, a little there, and before I knew it . . ."

He glanced at her. His sad, hound-dog smile ripped at her heart.

"Say something! Scream! Shout! Beat me," she demanded. "Anything but be nice."

"Would it do any good?" he asked. "It sounds to me like you're doing enough for both of us."

Kari stared straight ahead at the dashboard. "I wouldn't have blamed you if you refused to come for me."

"Kari, 'for better, for worse,' remember? You're my wife and I love you," he reminded. "Besides, if I rake you over the coals for what happened, next time, you might hesitate to call me."

"Next time? There's never going to be a next time."

Marc's silence throughout the rest of the drive home unnerved Kari. She knew he doubted her resolve, and she couldn't really blame him. "After all," she reasoned, "he can't know how determined I am. And I am determined!"

Chapter 12
A Time to Cast Away

Kari pushed her carefully folded sheets to one side of the linen-closet shelf. Her hand touched the sought-after object. Sliding her fingers along the cool sides of the bottle, she grasped it about the neck, pulling it out from its hiding place. She paused, listening. Was Casey awake?

She waited until certain no one was around. Then, clasping the amber bottle to her chest, she scurried down the hall to the bathroom. There, under the sink, behind a stack of unopened toilet paper rolls, she located the tiny, weighted-bottomed shot glass.

She hated herself for her duplicity, for the charade she maintained. It wasn't that Kari hadn't meant to keep her promises to Marc. She meant every one of them. However, for reasons she couldn't explain even to herself, something within her had changed after the wedding shower escapade. She couldn't seem to maintain her vow not to drink. On the way to work, she would occasionally buy a bottle of scotch or a fifth of gin, then later, upon returning home after her shift, she'd hide it. The guilt she experienced over stashing liquor in every secret niche of the house wasn't as powerful as her craving for the beverage.

She justified her actions by saying she never drank around Casey, always waiting until her daughter was napping or out with Mom Wynters or Mindy.

Several times, she'd been forced to guzzle down an extra large swig of mouthwash from the bottle she kept in the cupboard beside the kitchen sink in order to avoid detection. Once, Mom Wynters arrived a half hour earlier than expected. Kari was certain the woman suspected her condition. Another time, Michael dropped off some garden produce unannounced. He eyed her suspiciously when she giggled at something he said that struck her funny.

To ensure her privacy, she moved her saloon upstairs to the bathroom. "No one will be able to sneak up on me in here," she reasoned.

Day after day, she teetered on the edge of sobriety, her brain either besotted by booze or besieged by blame. When sober, remorse compelled her to search her Bible for a way of escape. She repeated the promises over and over again. "If you seek Me with all your heart . . . I will never leave you nor forsake you. . . . Lo, I am with you always. Nothing can separate you from the love of God."

She longed for the innocent faith she once treasured. Instead, she felt nothing but a frigid emptiness. Her prayers seemed to bounce off the ceiling, back into her upturned face. She ached for the peace she'd enjoyed in the early days, when her love for her heavenly Father was clean and new.

She recalled her mother's battle and the resulting physical and spiritual defeat. "Have You deserted me, God, like You did Sheena?" she wailed, her accusations echoing off the walls surrounding her.

As her emotions fluctuated between silent fury and despair, the resulting inner turmoil spilled out onto family and friends. When Marc questioned her, she replied, "I've not been feeling well lately. I must be coming down with something."

When he suggested she make an appointment to see Dr. Williams, she snapped, "I don't need a country quack to relieve us of twenty dollars just to tell me to take a couple of aspirin and stay in bed for a day or two."

One hectic Thursday afternoon, after chasing the now-walking Casey about the house all morning, Kari put the little girl down for her nap, then rushed to pour herself her daily "mood elevator." Since Marc had said he was driving to Madison to pick up a part for the tractor and her in-laws were in Michigan visiting Shelly and her family, she decided to forego her usual precautions and enjoy the drink in the comfort of her living room.

With a bottle of Chardonnay in one hand and a wine glass in the other, she settled herself comfortably in the big chair. She filled her glass, then placed the bottle on the end table. Swietzer lay sleeping on the ottoman in front of her.

Her eyes rested momentarily on the closed Bible on the end table. Feeling rebellious, she reached down into the magazine rack on the other side of the chair and drew out a popular magazine to read, then settled back for a relaxing afternoon.

She ignored the persistent Swietzer rubbing against her legs. When the cat failed to receive the attention desired, he curled up and went to sleep. She hadn't read long, or so it seemed, when she heard a wail from upstairs. "Oh, for pity's sake, Casey," she muttered, pulling herself to her feet. "Can't I have a moment to myself?" Swietzer leaped off the footstool and bounded from the room.

The familiar sensation of spinning caused Kari to pause long enough to get her balance. She glanced down at the wine bottle. Over a third was gone. She shook her head, unable to remember just how many glasses she had poured.

Casey's cries intensified. Kari staggered into the hall, and by concentrating on each step, she made it to the top of the stairs and into the nursery. Her inebriation didn't prevent her from immediately recognizing the cause of Casey's agitation.

The little girl had managed the impossible. She'd climbed over the crib railing and was dangling by one foot from the side. Somehow the fitted crib sheet had wrapped itself around her ankle; the other end of the sheet still firmly clutched the corners of the mattress.

Kari rushed to the crib and lifted the hysterical child into her arms. Intent upon soothing Casey, Kari failed to hear Marc's truck pull up or hear him enter the house, call for her, and bound up the stairs and into the room.

"Kari, what's happened?" He rushed to her side.

Kari's face flushed as their eyes met. Immediately she knew he knew, not only of the baby's predicament, but also of her state of inebriation. In silent fury, he snatched Casey from Kari's arms and disentangled the baby's foot from the sheet. Without a word, he stormed from the house with

Casey, hopped into the truck, and disappeared down the driveway in a cloud of dust.

Somewhat sobered, she eased down the stairs and into the living room. From across the room, the partially empty wine bottle mocked her. From habit, she thought to hide it before he returned. "A little late for that," she snorted. "Talk about closing the barn door after the horse escapes. Or is it a cow that escapes?"

The roar of the truck's engine alerted her to her husband's return. Through the window she watched the vehicle screech to a halt in front of the walkway. Marc climbed out of the cab minus Casey and strode purposefully into the house.

She met him at the door. "Where's Casey? Where's my baby?" she demanded. "I suppose you ran straight to Mama, huh?"

"Casey is at the house with Mindy. I don't especially want my daughter to overhear what I have to say to her mother!"

Shocked at the vehemence in his voice, Kari took a step backward in self-defense.

"Sit down!" he ordered, pointing toward the sofa.

Kari lifted her chin defiantly. "You can't talk to—"

"I said, 'Sit down!' " He moved menacingly toward her.

Gathering as much dignity as she could muster, she obeyed.

"I've been as patient as I know how with you and your drinking," he began. "But I can't take it anymore. I won't spend the rest of my life worried each time I leave you alone with my child, that she might be in danger due to this stuff!" He swung his broad, calloused hand about and connected with the bottle on the end table. Kari jumped as the bottle crashed against the mantle above the stone fireplace, shattering into hundreds of pieces. Its contents splattered onto the stones, the wall beside it, and down onto the hearth below.

"Marc," Kari whimpered.

"I tried to convince you to get professional help. But no, self-sufficient little Kari refused to ask for help." His words pelted her senses with blizzard force. "I have had it! Do you understand?

"You think you're so clever, hiding your precious little

caches about the house. How stupid do you think I am?" He whirled about to face her, his upper lip curling in disgust. "How long have you been playing your little game of 'catch me if you can'? A month? Two months? Perhaps since the day you married me!"

"No, no, I—"

"I tried to take my dad's advice. 'Read the story of Hosea and Gomer, son. Go after her, love her back.' " She watched him shake his head as if struggling to shake free of his pain.

"Marc, I—"

"Spare me your vows and promises. It's too late for apologies. Right now, the very sound of your voice makes me cringe."

For a moment, Kari remained immobilized by his harsh indictment. Suddenly, when the horror of his words penetrated her shock, she burst into tears and fled upstairs to their bedroom. Instead of following her, he stormed from the house. She waited, expecting to hear the truck engine start. But all remained silent.

She threw herself onto the bed and curled into a tight little ball. Scalding tears trickled down her face. Too much pain, too much deception, too much anger, much too late. It was so quiet in the empty house that the silence itself almost had a sound. Slowly she stood up and surveyed the master bedroom. The translucent curtains fluttered in the breeze of the open window. She fluffed her down-filled pillow back into shape, then walked to the closet and removed her overnight case and a suitcase from the shelf.

Her fingers shook as she struggled to undo the clasps of the case. Too late—the saddest words in the English language. "Yes, maybe he's right. Maybe it is too late for us."

When she finished packing, she paused to take a last look about the room—the room she'd decorated with such loving care; the room she'd returned to as a bride, overflowing with love and joy; the room where their precious daughter had been conceived. Through a wall of tears, she stumbled down the stairs, picked up her purse and keys before heading out the front door.

Climbing into her car, she glanced toward the barn. For a moment, she thought she saw Marc's form in the doorway.

Slowly, as if a very old woman, she turned the key in the ignition. When no voice called to her from the barnyard, when no one came running to stop her departure, Kari reluctantly put the car into gear and drove down the long driveway.

"My baby. I've got to see my baby." Upon reaching the highway, she turned the car toward Marc's parents' home.

As if from habit, the car came to a stop in front of Mom and Dad Wynters' home. Kari hopped out and ran up the steps to the front door. Frantic, beyond reason, she burst into the parlor, where Mindy sat in the middle of the floor playing blocks with Casey. The sight of her frazzled, hysterical mother reaching for her frightened the already upset child.

Casey screamed and scrambled from Kari's outstretched arms into Mindy's. In horror, Kari watched her daughter bury her face in Mindy's shoulder, terrified of her own mother.

Kari shook her head violently. "No, no. Not you too," she screamed. "I am your mother. I love you."

The frightened baby burrowed deeper into the arms of her aunt. Shattered beyond words, Kari rose to her feet and left the house.

With the child clinging to her neck, Mindy rushed after Kari. "No, don't leave. Casey didn't mean anything. You startled her. That's all."

With stiff, androidlike movements, Kari climbed back into the vehicle, closing the door behind her. Her eyes, though wide open from terror, focused on nothing at all as she drove away—away from Marc, from her child, from her home, away from the Wynters, the only family she'd ever known.

Chapter 13

A Time of Despair

Kari twisted and untwisted the facial tissue in her hands until a mottled layer of lint specks coated the lap of her navy skirt. "So," she continued, "I really could use full-time employment now."

Mrs. Perkins, the hospital's nursing supervisor, studied Kari's face. "Kari, is there something you aren't telling me that I should know? I'm here for more than just arranging work schedules for my nurses, you know. I'm here to help whenever I can."

Kari dropped her gaze to the floor. "I . . . I . . . I don't know where to begin." She took a deep breath. "Marc and I are having some difficulties right now and need a break from one another."

"In my day, when trouble came, marriage partners drew together, not apart. Sorry, I don't mean to be judgmental." The gray-haired woman leaned back in the desk chair and shook her head. "What about your baby, Casey, isn't it?"

"Since I will need to work full time, it seemed wiser for her to stay with her father. He's making arrangements with his mother and sister for Casey's care." Kari's face flushed uncomfortably. "And it's not like I'm moving out of state or something. I'll be living here in Beaver Dam, a little more than ten miles away."

"Yes, well . . ." The older woman leaned forward, placing her elbows on the broad walnut-veneer desktop. Her lips pursed as she matched finger for finger on her two hands. "I would dearly love to deny your request—tell you to go home to your husband and work out your problems. Unfortunately, I have a

80

nursing schedule to fill. And I desperately need a good nurse on the graveyard shift."

Kari straightened her shoulders; her eyes sparkled in anticipation.

"It's in intensive care. Have you ever worked there?"

"No, but I'm sure I can handle it. And I'd be glad to take whatever classes necessary to upgrade my skills."

Mrs. Perkins nodded and smiled. Her smile couldn't displace the sadness evident in her pale gray eyes. "The University of Wisconsin offers an excellent program." She bit the corner of her lip and scowled. "Look, I'm not sure I'm doing you any favors by making it so easy for you to leave your family."

"Believe me, leaving Marc and Casey has been far from easy. It's the most difficult thing I've ever had to do. And, perhaps you are helping our marriage instead of hurting it," Kari suggested. "If you hadn't had an opening for me, I would have had to move to Madison, or perhaps return to Chicago to find work."

"Thanks, I needed that to salve my conscience a bit. OK, you have the job. We'll work out your training schedule later." The woman smiled. "But, as you know, working in the intensive care unit is more stressful than on regular floors. There's no margin for error when any case could develop into a life-and-death situation."

Kari couldn't believe her luck. "Maybe my life will straighten out after all," she thought. "Working nights will give me days to spend with Casey without Marc's hovering presence and will give me time to decide where to go from here."

Kari adjusted to the routine of ICU with ease. After making arrangements to share living expenses with Bitsy, she settled into a pattern that both satisfied and disturbed her. For a time, she found a certain pleasure in pleasing only herself for a change. Yet, after each visit with Casey, she mourned having missed the day-by-day changes occurring in the little girl's life. And Marc, even hearing his name caused more pain than she allowed herself to admit.

The family studiously avoided mentioning him when she went to see the baby. Michael avoided her as much as his brother did. Mom and Dad acted as kind and solicitous as ever. But whenever Mindy managed to get Kari away from the rest of the family, she dropped little bits of information about her older brother, always ending with, "He still loves you a lot, you know." Secretly, Kari treasured these confidences.

She threw herself into her job. Working the night shift at such a critical position prevented the lonely predawn hours from overpowering her. The classwork and the forty-five mile drive to her university classes in Madison filled her days. On weekends, Kari volunteered for extra duty whenever possible.

"See," she told herself one evening as she finished piling her hair into her customary French twist, "I knew I could handle my life without Marc or a drug counselor. And that's, I might add, while enjoying an occasional pick-me-up!" The woman in the mirror smiled a plastic beauty-contestant smile. Kari tilted her nose a little higher, added a last poof of hairspray, and hurried to work.

There had been times, if she'd dared to admit, when her little pick-me-up left her more strung out than she'd planned. As a nurse, she knew she'd made errors due more to the alcohol content in her blood than to her inexperience on the unit. She had missed one or two classes because, even while slightly tipsy, she couldn't bring herself to drink, then drive. She'd worked too many hours in the emergency room as a student nurse to make that mistake.

With Kari working night shift and Bitsy on the evening shift, they saw little of one another. Either Kari was rushing to classes or Bitsy was late for work.

One morning, as Kari stumbled home from work, her eyes bloodshot and her nose red, Bitsy asked, "What's with you? You look terrible."

"I think I've got the flu," she groaned, "and I have a midterm this afternoon. I'm getting too old for this co-ed stuff," she sniffled. The long hours of work, classes, and study drained Kari more than she imagined possible. "If I can just study this morning and take that test, then I can afford to give in to this thing. I already told Mrs. Perkins I was sick and wouldn't be in tonight."

"After working all last night?" Bitsy shook her head. "Well, at least you did something right."

Kari staggered into the bathroom and started her shower.

Bitsy knocked on the closed door. "Do you want me to call a doctor?"

"Can't afford it," Kari called over the noise of the spray. "I'll take a few aspirins and go to bed after class."

"I saw Marc at the supermarket yesterday," Bitsy volunteered. "He said to tell you hi."

Kari paused. "So you told me."

"He's attending some Al-Anon meetings here in town—you know, the meetings for relatives of alcoholics. I told him to stop by the apartment sometime, that you'd love to see him."

"Give it up, Bitsy," Kari warned. She listened as Bitsy stomped off to her own room.

Kari dried off, wrapped herself in her comfortable, old bathrobe, took the medication, and headed for her room. Once there, she perched herself in the middle of her bed to study. "Hmm," she muttered, "let's start with the most tedious of the lot."

As she reached for one particularly thick book from the stack of books beside her bed, her gaze rested on the two radiant faces in the photo atop her night stand—she and Marc on their wedding day. The camera had captured the innocent glow in her face and an almost reverent devotion in Marc's eyes as he gazed down at her. She bit her lip and turned the frame toward the wall.

"OK, Kari Gerard Wynters, get busy." She coughed; her head pounded. She opened the book and stared at the blurring letters and illustrations on the pages before her. Leaning back against her pillows, she finally admitted, "With this headache, my eyes just won't focus. Maybe a short nap will help—give the pills time to work." She curled up and fell asleep.

An irritating knock on the bedroom door awakened Kari. Bitsy stuck her head inside the room. "It's two forty-five. I wanted to be sure you don't need something before I left for the hospital."

"Two forty-five!" Kari leaped from the bed and grabbed the alarm clock from the night stand. "It can't be! I have a class in less than an hour—the test! Oh, no," she wailed.

"You shouldn't be going anywhere." Bitsy entered the room

and felt Kari's forehead. "Your face is still flushed. Here, let me see if your fever has dropped any."

"I don't have time for this, mother hen. Neither do you. See you later."

Kari threw off her robe and slipped into her jeans and a university sweat shirt. Tying her sneakers and brushing her frizzed curls almost simultaneously, she grabbed her blue denim jacket and dashed from the apartment.

One hour later, she skidded to a halt just inside the classroom door. The class was already in session. Sheepishly, she simpered an apology for being tardy and sat down in the nearest empty seat.

She glanced through the test booklet on the desk before her. Nothing made sense to her. It might as well have been written in Yiddish, for all she knew. She ran her hand distractedly through her tousled hair.

"Oh, Father," she whispered, more from habit than design, "I really blew it this time. I suppose it would be asking too much for You to bail me out."

One by one, the other students handed in their completed test papers and exited the room until only she and the instructor remained. Knowing there was little to be said, Kari dropped the test on the teacher's desk and left.

Throughout the return drive to Beaver Dam, she berated herself, first for being sick, second for falling asleep, third for even thinking she could do the course work itself. She thought about Marc. "Flat on my face—won't that make you happy?" Her anger and guilt mingled with her discouragement, creating a lethal cocktail of self-destruction.

By the time she entered the empty apartment, her course of action was determined. Kari strode purposefully toward the liquor cabinet. She poured and swallowed her favorite gin before she even removed her jacket. Without thinking, she switched on the television.

The bottle emptied two drinks later, Kari lay sprawled across the sofa, the evening news blaring from the television.

Surrealistic, distorted faces of family and friends tortured her dreams. She struggled to escape the hideous images bombarding her. "I've got to wake up," she insisted. Stirring from the couch, she stumbled into the bathroom and splashed water on her face. She stared at herself in the mirror and gasped. Instead of her smooth, unlined complexion, she saw her mother's ravaged face. Instead of her own sparkling eyes staring back at her, she saw Sheena's empty, bloodshot eyes. Somewhere in the last few hours, she had become her mother. In irritation, she pushed the thought from her mind. "I look terrible! I need a drink."

After searching the entire apartment and finding no alcohol, Kari decided to walk the four blocks to a store for more. "The fresh air will do me good."

Kari buttoned the top button of her jacket and started out. She strolled by the parked automobiles lining the curb. The last of the small-town commuters had reached home, leaving only the occasional car to drive by. A biting wind whipped across her face, alerting her to the approach of winter. She grinned and braced herself against it. "The holidays will soon be here," she thought, "my favorite time of year—or at least, was . . ."

She entered the store and made her purchase. Stepping out onto the darkened sidewalk, she stuffed the brown paper sack containing the gin bottle under her arm and headed for home.

Kari hadn't walked more than twenty feet when she sensed someone following her. Frightened, she glanced over her shoulder in time to see the shadow of a man disappear in a doorway. She walked faster; so did the man. She crossed to the other side of the street. He followed. By the sound of his footsteps, she knew he was moving closer, much closer. Terrified, she broke into a dead run.

When she reached her block, she realized she was returning to an empty apartment. Yet, where else could she run? She darted diagonally across the intersection. Suddenly, her toe caught on the drain grating, plunging her face down onto the concrete. Her package rolled from her side, unharmed.

Stunned, Kari expected at any moment to feel the death grip of her attacker around her throat. She lifted her eyes long enough to catch the blur of a man run past her and down the street after her pursuer. As she struggled to stand up, two strong and familiar arms encircled her waist, lifting her to her feet.

"Marc? What are you doing here?" she cried.

"Rescuing a damsel in distress," he gasped, out of breath from the chase. "I'm afraid the punk got away. Are you all right?"

Kari glanced down at her ripped blue jeans and her mud-splattered jacket. Already her bruised knees ached.

"I . . . I . . . I think so," she whispered, reaching for the package still lying on the sidewalk. As she straightened up, she glanced at Marc. His knowing gaze traveled from her face to the bag and to her face again. Turning away, Kari swayed.

Immediately Marc's arms were around her, supporting her. "You're still shaking."

He helped her up the stairs into the apartment. "Why don't you take a little nap. I'll sit here and read and then fix you a cup of hot chocolate," he suggested.

After napping for almost an hour she felt less shaky, and her thoughts were less fuzzy again. She found Marc in front of the stove, stirring a pan of milk. Somehow it seemed so right to have Marc beside her, helping her, giving her strength.

"Do you feel better?"

"Marc, you never answered my question. What are you doing here?"

He looked up from the milk. "Didn't Bitsy tell you I was coming over?"

Kari shook her head.

"Well," he began, "to tell the truth, Bitsy called me from the hospital. She said that you were sick with the flu. She asked me to check on you."

"Bitsy . . ." Kari growled.

"It's lucky I did, huh?" Marc dipped a spoon into the pan and lifted it to his lips. "Ouch! I guess it's hot enough."

Kari giggled and sat down across the table from where he stood. "I do appreciate your help tonight, honest."

They maintained a strained silence while they drank the hot chocolate. Without warning, their eyes met. Marc reached across the table and captured her hands. "Come home, Kari, I miss you so much."

"I miss you too, Marc—more than you can know." Kari struggled to answer.

"Casey and I need you. We love you."

Kari gulped back her tears. "Marc, you said . . ."

Marc caressed the fingers of one hand, studying each line and crease. "I said a lot of things I shouldn't have. We both did. Forgive me?"

Kari glanced over at the brown paper bag near the sink. "What are the conditions?" Marc spotted the object of her attention.

"Kari, I was wrong about a lot of things. I've learned a lot since you left."

"Yes," Kari glowered, "the meetings."

"It was at those meetings I stopped blaming you and realized alcoholism isn't just a weak will but a genuine sickness needing medical treatment."

"Marc, I—"

"That's not all I've learned. With the help of Mom and Shelly, I now know that you can be a loving wife, a terrific mother, and a great nurse all at the same time. I guess I was threatened by your need to have a part of you that I did not share."

Kari stared in wonder. "Shelly?"

"But there is one thing you can't do, and that's drink. It will kill you." Marc released one of her hands and tilted her chin up to face him. "I love you too much to stand for that. I won't enable you to destroy yourself. You need professional help."

Kari jerked free from his touch. "So we're back to square one," Kari responded defensively. "Look, I've been doing just fine without the help . . ."

Marc's shoulders slumped forward. "As you wish."

Slowly, as if carrying the weight of eternity on his shoulders, Marc rose to his feet. "Kari, I think I'd better go. By the way, I need to run down to the truck after a package Mindy sent along, just in case you didn't choose to come home with me."

Stunned by his abrupt exit, Kari leaned against the sink for support. Before she could compose her confused emotions, Marc had returned.

"Here." He set the small travel case on the table and turned to leave. "Kari, please—if you ever need me for anything, if ever you want to come home to Casey and me, just call. I'll always be there for you." And he was gone.

Chapter 14

A Time for Healing

Kari remained immobile long after the sound of Marc's footsteps receded into the night. Why hadn't he argued with her? Why hadn't he tried a little harder to convince her to return home with him? Marc had changed, and she wasn't too sure she liked the changes.

Her head ached from the flu symptoms, and now, from her latest binge. *If he doesn't care any more than that, I guess he doesn't care enough,* she decided. Snatching the gin bottle from the bag, she uncapped it and lifted it to her lips. The reflection of this action in the window over the sink caught her attention. "Have you sunk so far," she questioned herself, "to drink straight from a bottle like the lowest street wino?" With deliberate motion, she placed the bottle on the counter and turned away.

She noticed the travel case in the middle of the table, and her curiosity was whetted. Opening it, the first item she spotted was her Bible. She lifted it from the case. A strange warmth filled her as she caressed its rough-textured cover. Reverently, she leafed through its pages. Bright yellow marking highlighted favorite passages. She paused at Jeremiah 31: "I have loved you with an *everlasting* love; I have drawn you with loving-kindness. I will *build you up again* and you will be rebuilt, O Virgin Israel." Key words had been underlined.

Remorse, with the force of a tidal wave, flooded over her. She crumbled to the floor. "Oh, Father, what have I done? Where did I lose my way?"

She sobbed until a dry ache behind her eyes replaced the

salty tears. Clutching the book to her chest, she arose and staggered to her room. "Please, Lord, show me the way. Show me what You'd have me do."

Long into the night, she read, prayed, then read some more. Time and again, her mind returned to the solution she had heard the most—get professional help. When she finally surrendered, she fell, exhausted, into the first peaceful sleep she'd experienced in months.

The first Alcoholics Anonymous meeting was a nightmare for Kari.

As she glanced about the scruffy little lodge hall at the people assembled, she shook her head. She'd seen these seedy-looking people slink in and out of her mother's life for years. "What am I doing? I don't belong here." Before she could slip out the door, a large friendly woman in her mid-forties grabbed Kari's arm.

"Hi, I'm Mabel. Is this your first visit to AA?"

Kari reddened. "Uh, yes."

"Well, don't be shy." She led a reluctant Kari to an empty folding chair. "The first visit is the hardest, you know. It gets easier."

"It would have to," Kari mumbled.

Kari hated every minute of the meeting. Hearing each member introduce himself, saying his first name, then admitting to being an alcoholic grated on her. Her conscious brain fought against the label. "I'm not an alcoholic. I'm not an alcoholic!" Yet, as each person shared his story and experience, she couldn't deny the similarities she saw to her own drinking habits. She did appreciate it when the members spoke of needing a Higher Power.

After several visits, Kari decided to tell her story. "Hi, my name is Kari, and I'm an alcoholic. I am also the daughter and granddaughter of alcoholics." Tears filled her eyes as she recited the events leading to her alcohol addiction. When she finished she felt cleansed, free for the first time in months.

The week preceding Thanksgiving, Mom Wynters called, inviting Kari to the family gathering. "We'd love to have you with us, especially Casey."

Kari wanted so much to say Yes, but she had so many battles to fight. The emotions raised by Marc's presence would only complicate the issues. Was she ready? She decided not. Until the war was won, she must wait.

"I'm sorry, Mom; it would be better if I stay away a while longer. Give my love to Casey—and to Marc." Before she could change her mind, she hung up.

Either by miracle or the kindness of her instructor at the university, Kari passed her class. She didn't know which. But she did appreciate not having to attend classes anymore. To avoid the temptation to sit down in front of the television with her favorite bottle of Canadian whiskey, Kari began taking long drives in her car, usually ending at Beaver Dam Lake. With Bible in hand, she'd stroll down by the water, reciting by memory the latest promises she'd uncovered. Once or twice she thought she saw Marc's truck cruise through the parking area. But by the time she reached her car, whoever it was had already driven away.

She longed to return to Marc, but somehow she knew she had to fight the battle for her sake, not for Marc's or even for Casey's, but for Kari's. She discovered as she searched deep inside herself that she'd spent her entire life being a "good girl," trying to please everyone but herself. She'd lived her early years playing mama and nursemaid to Sheena. She'd become a Christian partly because she didn't want to disappoint Amanda. She learned the requirements for becoming a good homemaker to please Mom Wynters. She'd performed the role of farmer's wife for Marc. Slipping into the responsibilities of mother to Casey had been the most natural step to complete the cycle.

"Where is Kari in all of this?" she asked herself. "I can't go back to Marc until I know. It wouldn't be fair to either of us," she decided. "It's one thing to be stubbornly self-sufficient, but it's something entirely different to be strong of mind and character."

She found working in intensive care rewarding except when a patient died. One night, in the middle of her shift, a two-year-old boy, who had been waiting for a kidney transplant, passed away. A favorite of the hospital staff, the child died just hours before the scheduled transfer to the university hospital for the surgery.

The rest of the night, the nursing staff moved about the unit in a trance. By the time the morning team arrived, Kari felt her nerves would snap. As she drove from the hospital parking lot, she thought, "I need a drink—just one, a pick-me-up." She recognized and tried to dispel the danger signals. But Christmas was everywhere.

Garlands of tinsel and glitter draped across the streets reminded Kari of the approaching Christmas holiday. "Christmas spirit?" she mused. "Not much Christmas spirit around knowing one very precious little boy will never see another Christmas."

Upon reaching the apartment, she immediately dialed Mabel, her AA partner. A recording machine answered.

"I'm sorry. I can't come to the phone right now." Disgusted, Kari hung up. She wandered about the apartment, ending up in front of Bitsy's liquor cabinet.

"Just once. No one will be hurt. No one needs to know," she reasoned. She opened the doors and reached in. Her fingers touched the cool, slick surface of a gin bottle. Suddenly, an image of Casey running toward her with arms outstretched flashed through Kari's mind. She pulled her hand from the bottle as if bitten by a snake.

"No!" she shouted. "I can't. I won't." Remembering Marc's last words to her, she picked up the phone and dialed. The telephone rang, once, twice, three times. On the fourth ring, Mindy answered.

"Wynters' residence, Mindy speaking."

"Hello, Mindy. This is Kari. Is Marc there?"

The girl's voice leaped an octave. "Kari? No, no Marc's not here right now. Are you OK? You sound kinda' funny."

"I'm fine," she admitted. "I was just hoping. . . . Oh well, I gotta go. Give Casey my love." Kari hung up before Mindy could say anything more.

"Now what?" she asked herself. "So much for 'always being there.' Hey, wait a minute." She whirled about. "You're not alone, remember?" She ran for her Bible and flipped the pages as quickly as possible to Hebrews 13:5.

"Never will I leave you; never will I forsake you." Suddenly she knew. After months of conflict, a profound truth struggled to be born within her mind. In a thunderclap of clarity, she realized her true identity and worth as a human being didn't rest in the roles she played—in her success as a wife, a mother, even as a nurse. Her value didn't depend on maintaining an energy-depleting schedule of community service or church responsibilities. As important as each role might be, the Kari that mattered most was Kari Elaine Gerard Wynters, daughter of the King of the Universe. This was her source of strength. This was her guarantee for success. This was her reason for being.

It sounded so corny, yet unbelievably wise—simple, yet profound. She laughed. She cried. She ached to share her thoughts with Marc. Where could he be? She considered showing up on his doorstep, unannounced.

Twirling excitedly about the room like a preteen prancing about in her first party dress, Kari announced, "I've got to get out of here—away from all temptation!" She grabbed her Bible, her purse, and coat. But first, she'd drive to the lake— their lake.

Dry leaves crumbled beneath her feet as she strolled along the shoreline. She came to a fallen log and sat down. Little patches of ice formed here and there on the surface of the water, attesting to the cold nights. The wild ducks and geese had long since winged their way south. Only the sound of the winds whistling through the bare branches broke the stillness.

"Thank You, Lord. Thank You. Your prodigal daughter is ready to go home, if You can convince my husband to take me back."

For some time, she gazed about the empty park, allowing her new-found peace to rejuvenate her depleted resources. Suddenly, she stood up.

"I'm going home!" she announced aloud. "I'm taking Marc at his word."

Kari marched up the grassy slope to the parking lot, jumped into her car, and drove as fast as she dared back to the apartment. "First, I'll pack my things, then go home where I belong. And if Marc has a problem with it, we'll just have to work it out later."

She pulled alongside the curb in front of the apartment complex. Kari bounded up the stairs and to her apartment.

She flung the door wide open and screeched to a halt. Her mouth gaped open, and her cheeks reddened when she suddenly found herself face-to-face with the third button of a well-fitted, blue denim jacket. Slowly Kari lifted her startled eyes to face the grinning, dimpled blond giant of a man—the man she loved.

"Hi, honey, I was just coming to find you."

"What are you doing here?" Kari babbled.

He tipped his head questioningly to one side. "Mindy said you called."

"Oh-oh-oh, bless her little interfering heart." Kari threw herself into his startled arms. Instantly, the familiar warmth from his arms held her so tightly she gasped for air. Marc groaned and buried his face in her tousled hair.

Minutes ticked by before either dared break the physical bond they'd hungered for so long. Then holding her at arms' length, he searched her face for the answer to the question yet unasked. "Kari, honey. Does this mean you're ready to come home?"

"Ready and eager," she replied, lifting her gaze to meet his, "if you'll have me."

"If I'll have you?" He stared, incredulous. Tears streamed unbidden down his strong, bronzed face. "Woman, you are bone of my bone, flesh of my flesh. I am an empty shell of a man without you."

A haunting cry escaped Kari's throat as she touched his cheek in an effort to remove his tears. He caught her hand in his and kissed each finger with an urgency bordering on desperation. "If only," she thought, "I could wipe away the scars I inflicted as easily as I wipe away his tears."

As if reading her mind, Marc tenderly placed a kiss on her lips, followed by another and another, each becoming more insistent than the last.

"Wait," she cried, "we need to talk first. There are so many things I want to say to you before we—begin again. First, I am so, so sorry for the pain I've put you through."

Marc stepped back for a moment struggling to compose himself. "You're right. We owe it to one another and to Casey to be certain our problems can be resolved before risking more injury and pain."

Kari glanced about the room. "I don't want to talk here. Give me a few minutes to throw a few things into a suitcase."

"We could drive to the lake—if you'd like," Marc suggested, as Kari raced about the apartment collecting her belongings.

At the lake, Kari described the struggles and the discoveries she'd made since leaving home. "The most difficult reality for me was accepting that alcoholism really is a disease as real as cancer or heart trouble. I truly believed if I tried hard enough, I could defeat it. Instead, it defeated me." She snuggled closer under the protection of his arm. "That meant forgiving my mother and forgiving myself." Her voice broke. "You know, Marc, I will always be an alcoholic."

"I know, honey. I know." Marc's arm tightened around her shoulder as he told of the nightmare he'd been living since she'd gone. Silent tears flooded her face as she felt the pain and rejection he'd experienced. "It took a lot for me to realize that I had made some dumb mistakes too. I needed to learn that you weren't an appendage of me, ready to perform upon demand. I needed to allow you to be your own person."

They talked until the hazy winter sun disappeared behind the trees at the far side of the lake. Suddenly Kari bolted upright. "Marc, it's past time for evening chores. We'd better get home."

Marc laughed. "Michael's taking care of that."

At the mention of Marc's little brother, Kari shrank down into the seat.

"Don't worry," Marc encouraged, "he was eager to help out if it meant getting us back together again. He's had to change his share of diapers these last few months, too, you know."

Kari grew quiet for a moment.

"OK, what's going on in that wise little head of yours?"

"I wish I could erase all the pain I've caused. . . ."

"We've caused," he reminded.

"If only," she continued, "we could somehow begin again— all fresh and new."

A gleam entered Marc's eyes. Suddenly he started the truck and tore out of the parking lot.

"What are you doing?" Kari demanded. "Where are we going?"

He grinned but didn't speak. When he reached the main

intersection of town, he turned south instead of north. For the ten miles to the little town of Columbus, Kari continued to demand an explanation, but to no avail.

Stopping the truck beside the deserted train station in Columbus, he hopped from the cab, pulling her along behind. By the time they reached the concrete platform next to the tracks, Kari was laughing uncontrollably.

Grasping her shoulders, he turned her away from him. "Excuse me." He tapped her on the shoulder. "But you are Kari Gerard, aren't you?"

Kari turned slowly, a silly grin broadening across her face. "Marc, this is—"

"You look very much like the picture my Aunt Amanda sent. Come on, ask me who I am."

Noticing a lone ticket agent eyeing them suspiciously from the station's open doorway, Kari pushed Marc away. "I'm sorry, you must be mistaken—"

He scowled. "Hey, you're changing the script."

Arching one eyebrow, she continued. "My name is Mrs. Kari Wynters. And if you're smart, young man, you'll move on because my husband is meeting me here any moment. He won't take kindly to someone moving in on his wife."

When the concerned agent inched threateningly closer, the couple fell into each other's arms laughing.

The humor of the moment was interrupted by an unusually loud growl from Kari's stomach.

"My, my," Marc teased, "it sounds like either there's a wild beast loose within you or you're mighty hungry. Can I interest you in a meal in our local four-star diner?"

Kari's eyes sparkled at the mention of Duke's Diner. "Only if you will spring for the check."

Taking her arm in his, he started toward the illegally parked truck. "Not going dutch, Mrs. Wynters?" he teased.

"This time it's your treat all the way."

He paused, his mood shifting from levity to tenderness. "It will be a pleasure, a genuine pleasure, my dear Mrs. Wynters."

"He hath made everything beautiful in His time."